ANIMALS OF THE FOREST

&

ANIMALS DOING VERY HUMAN THINGS

COLORING BOOK

ANIMALS
Of The Forest

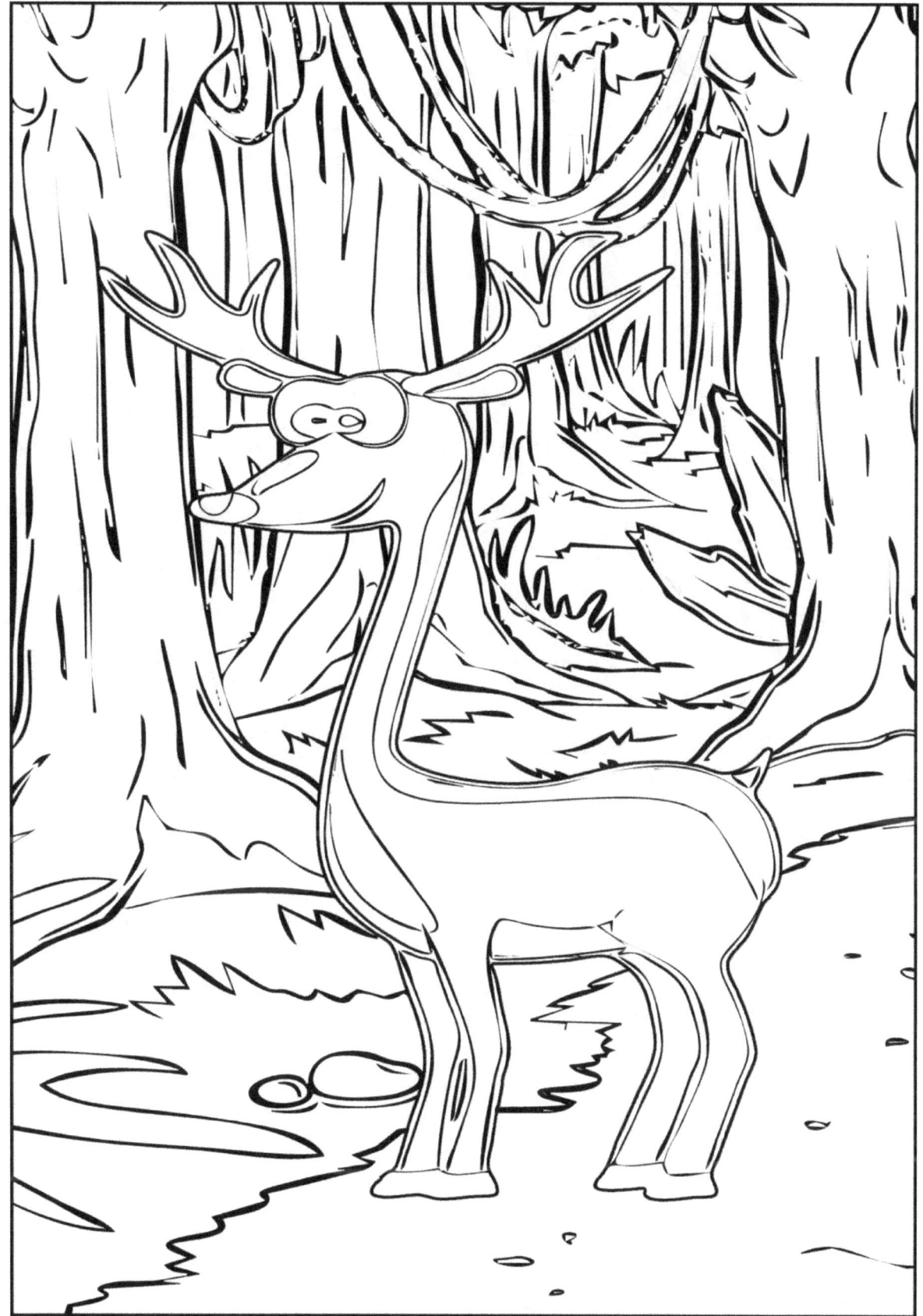

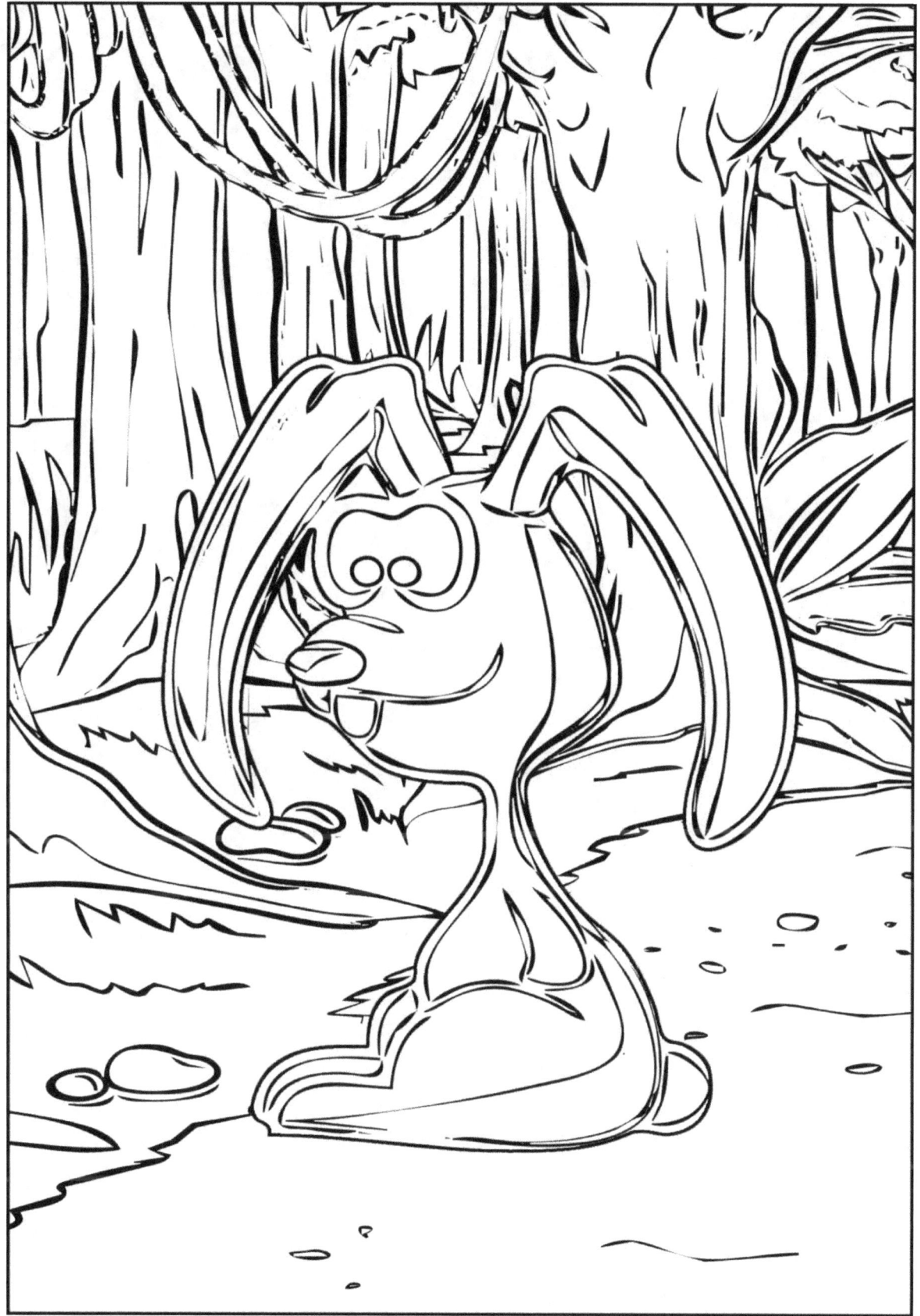

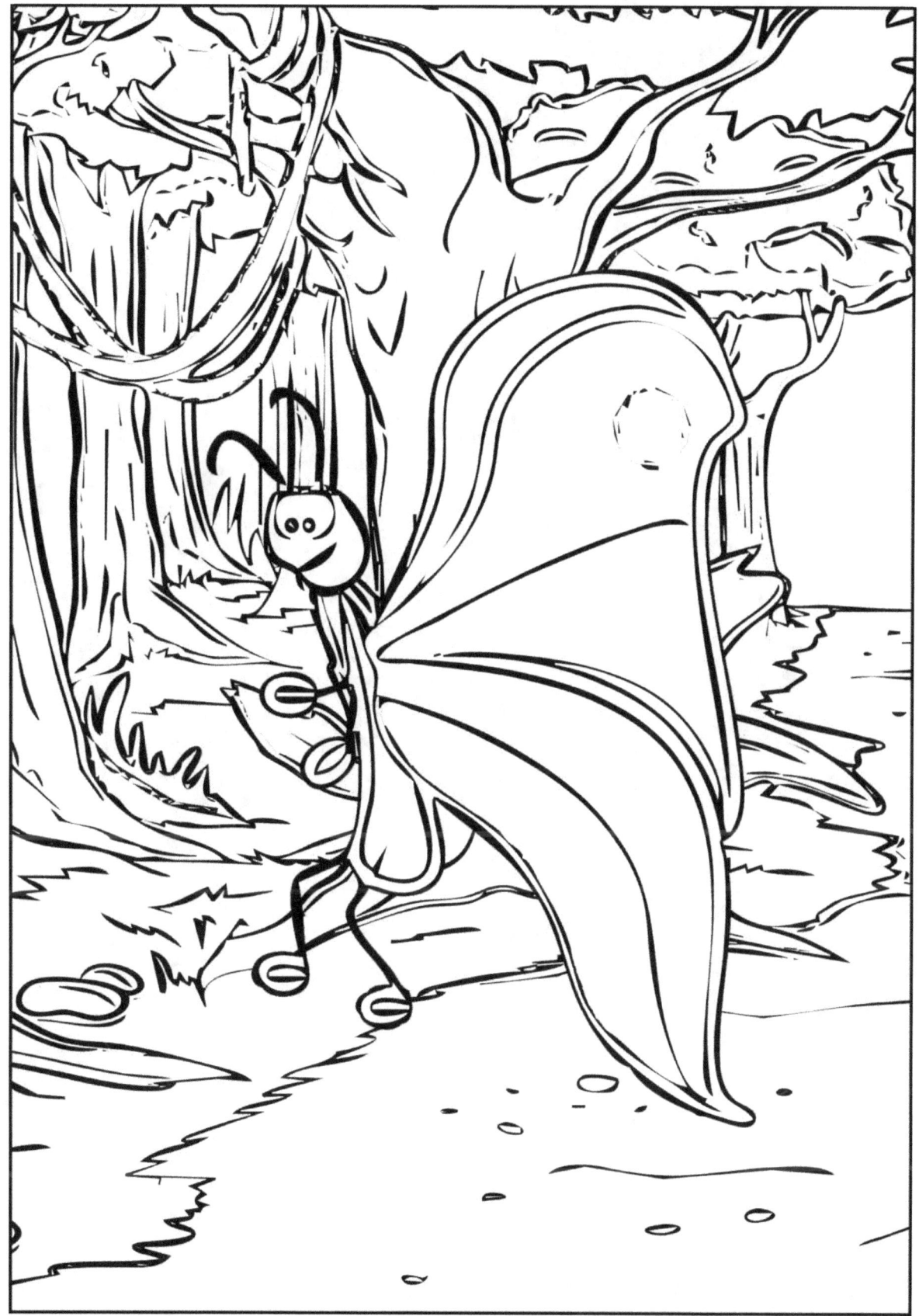

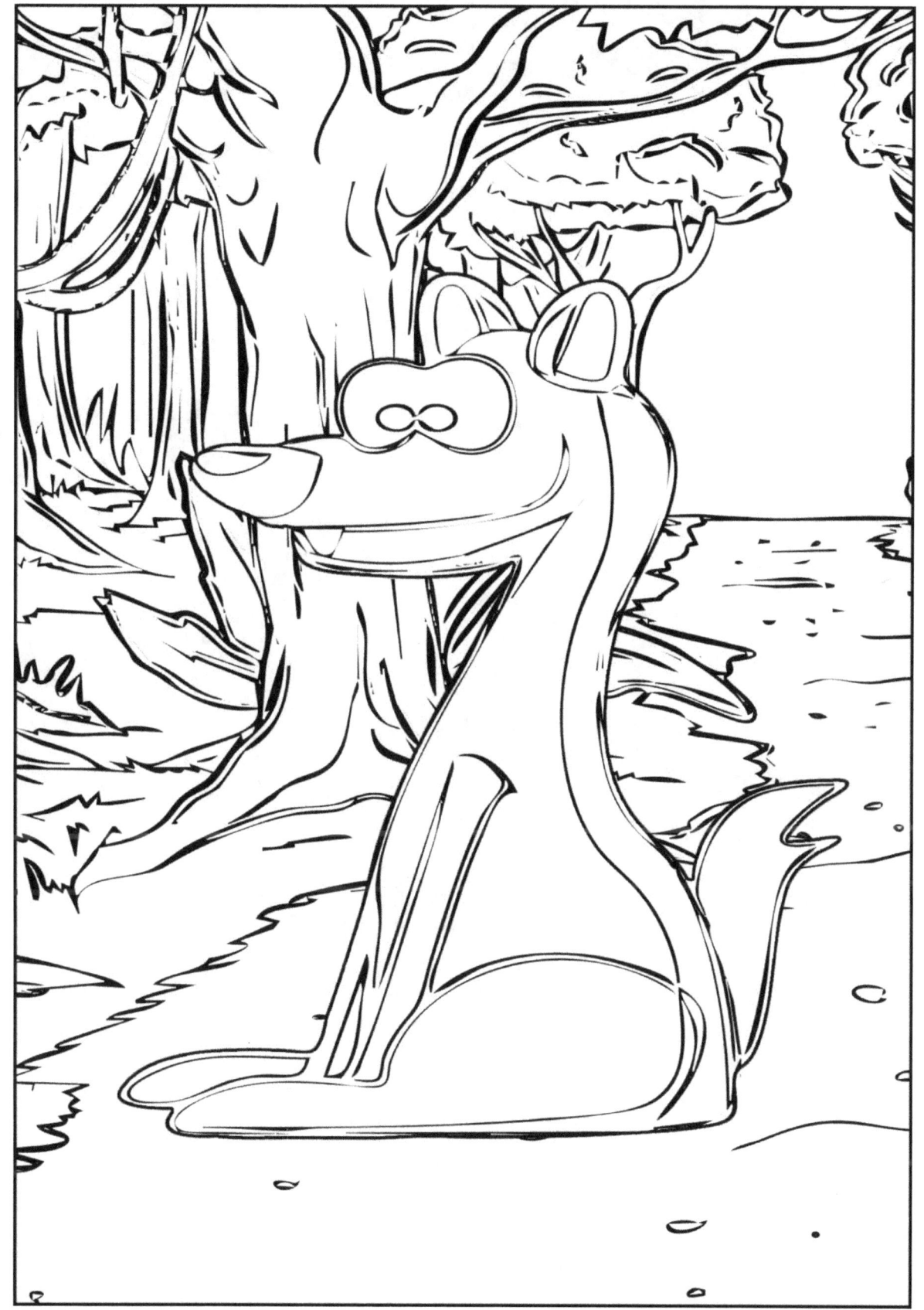

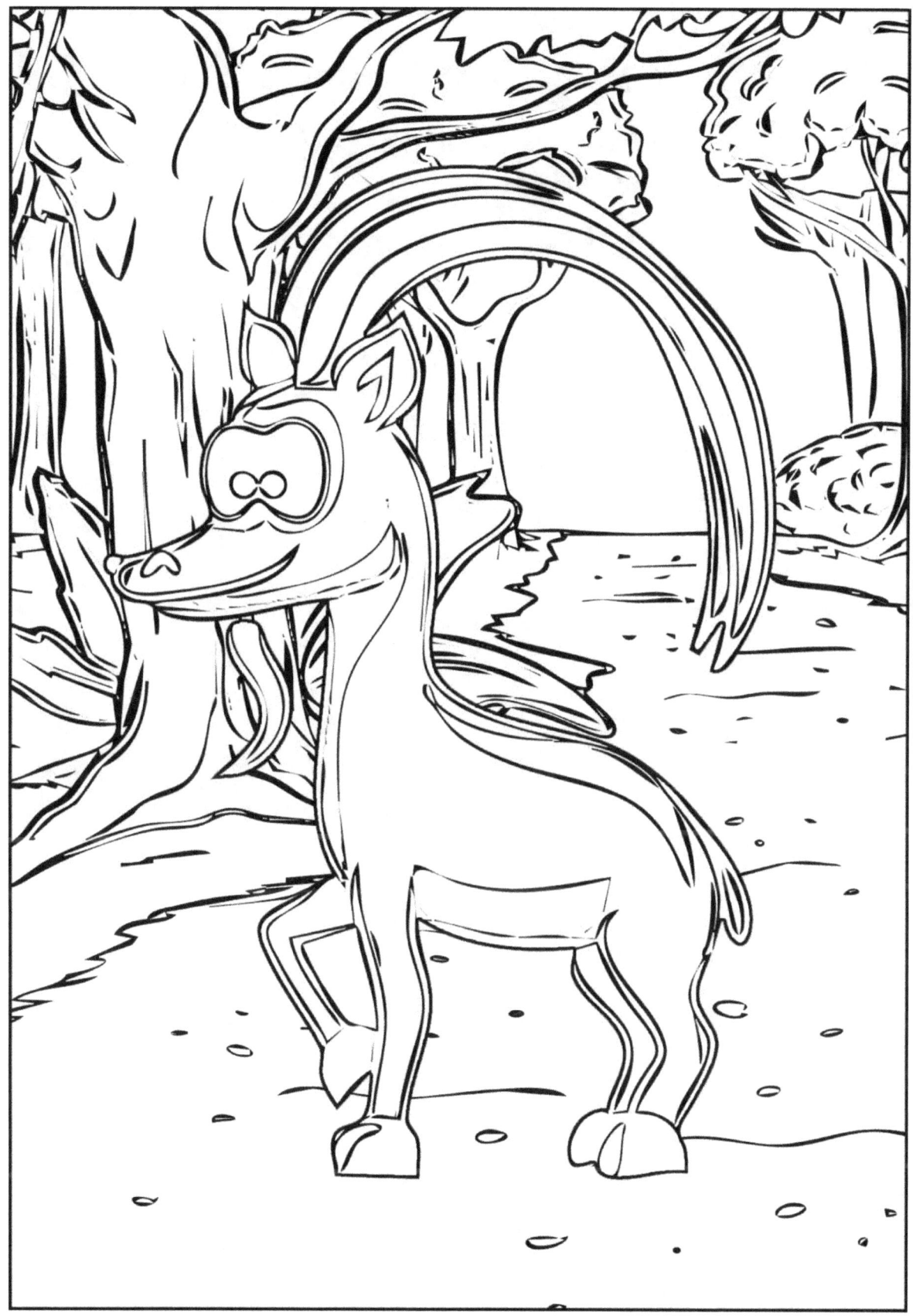

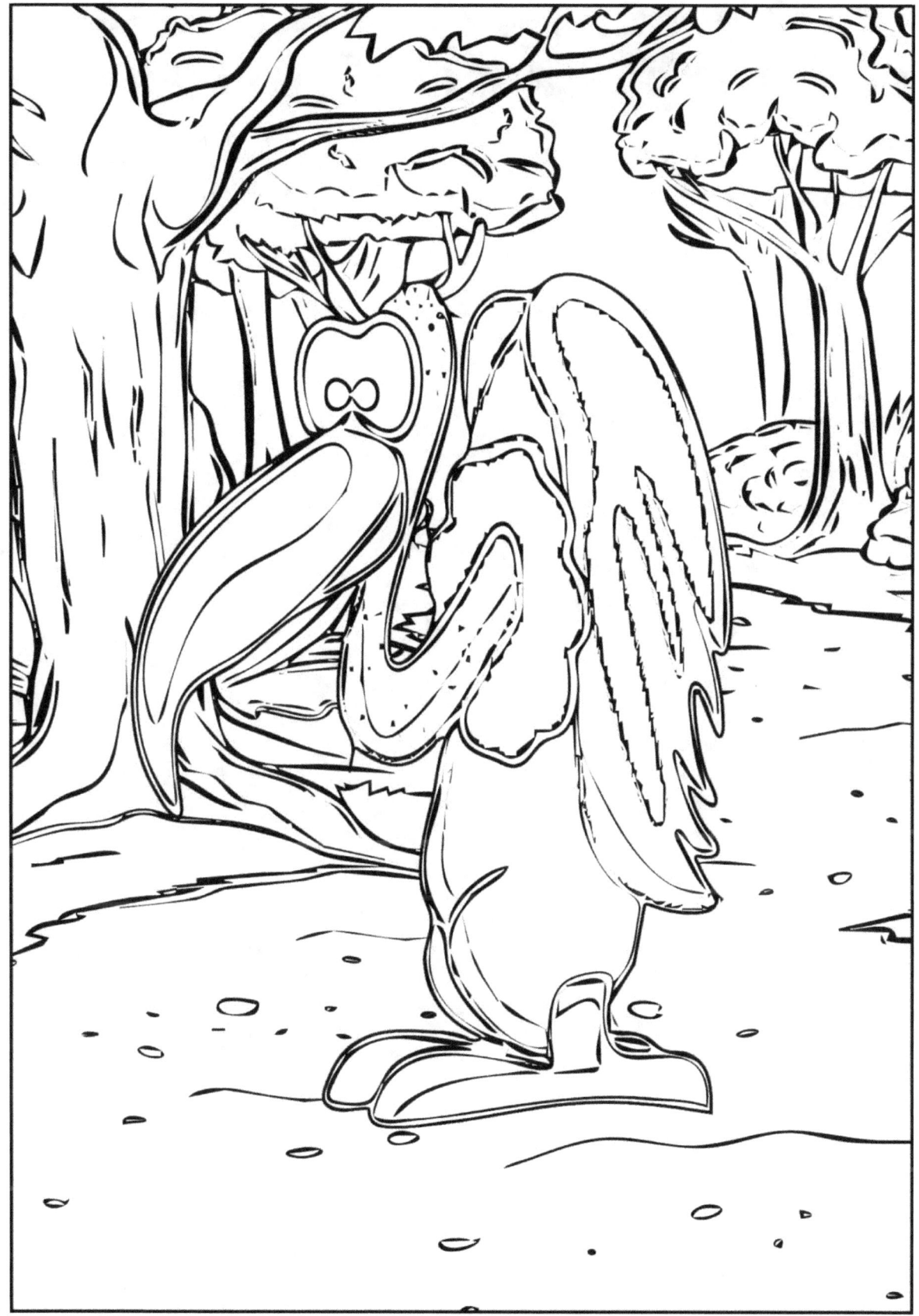

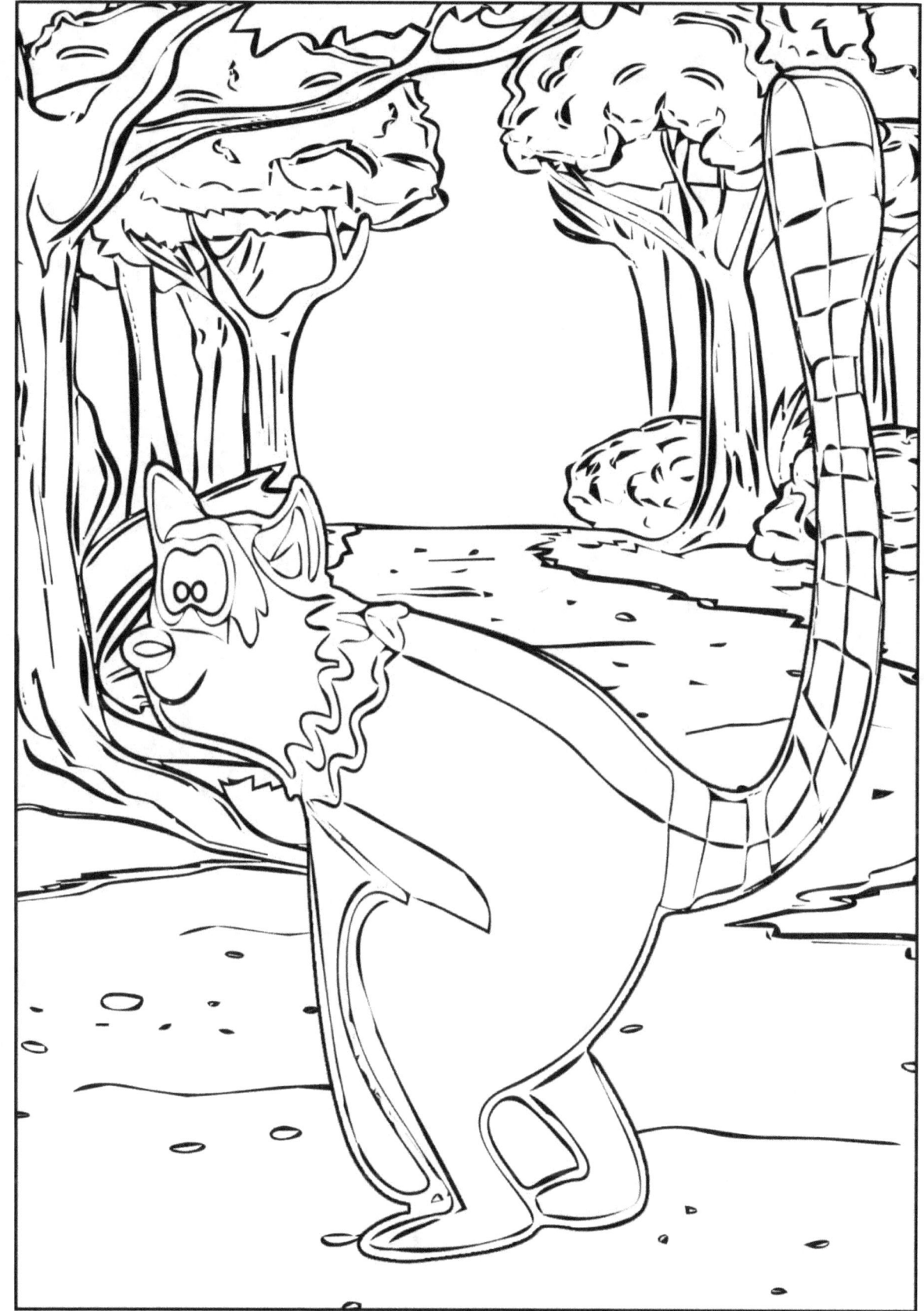

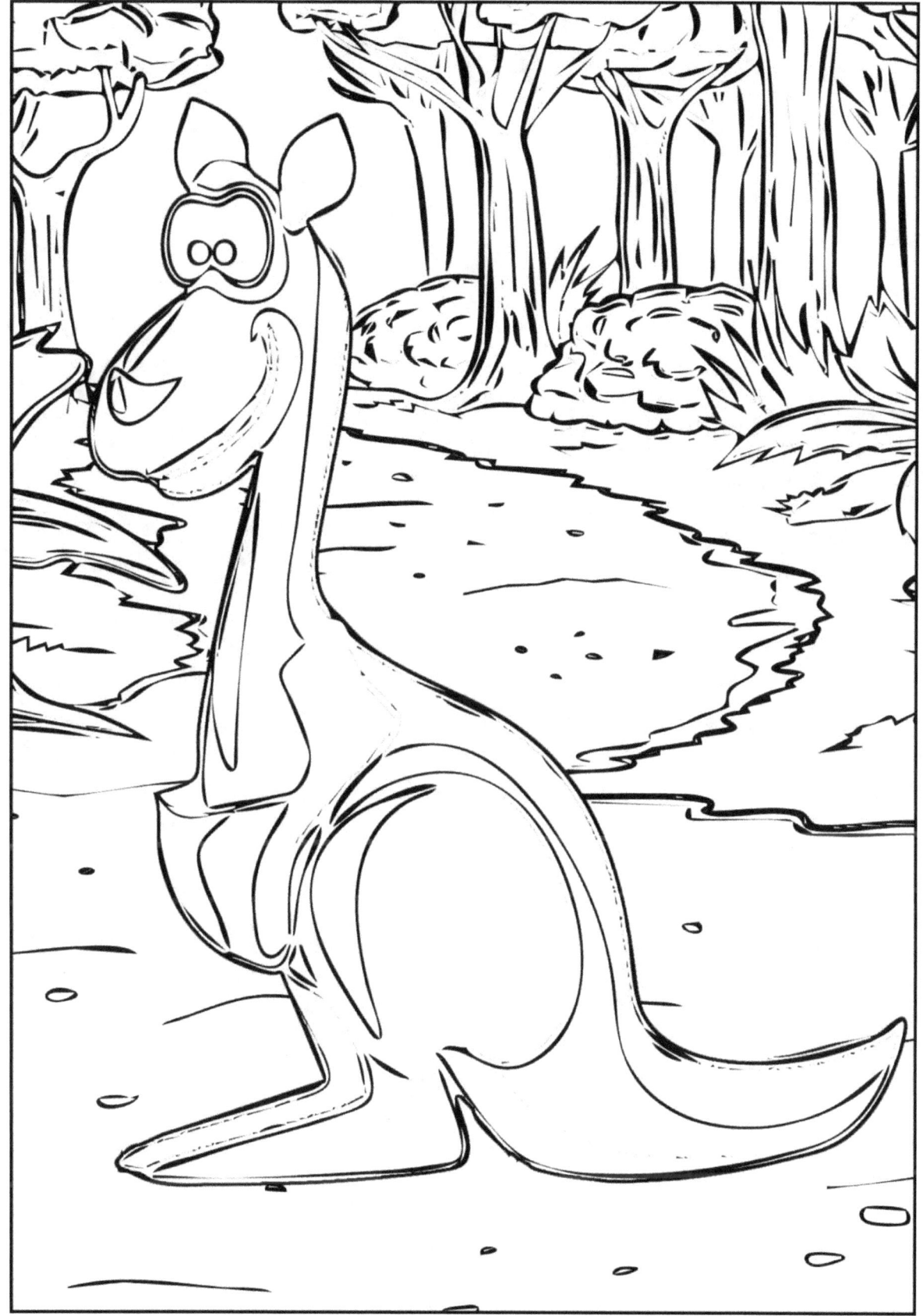

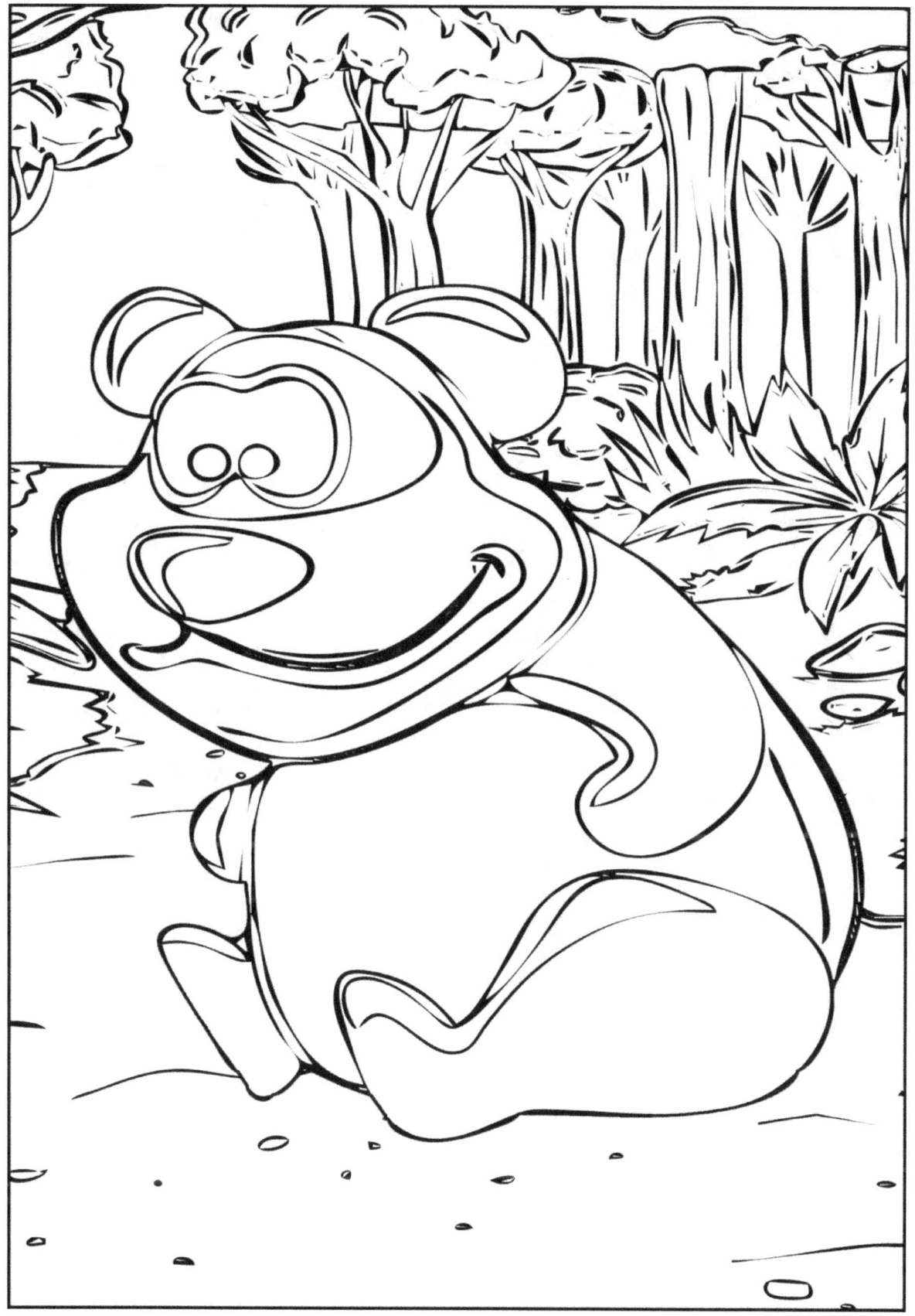

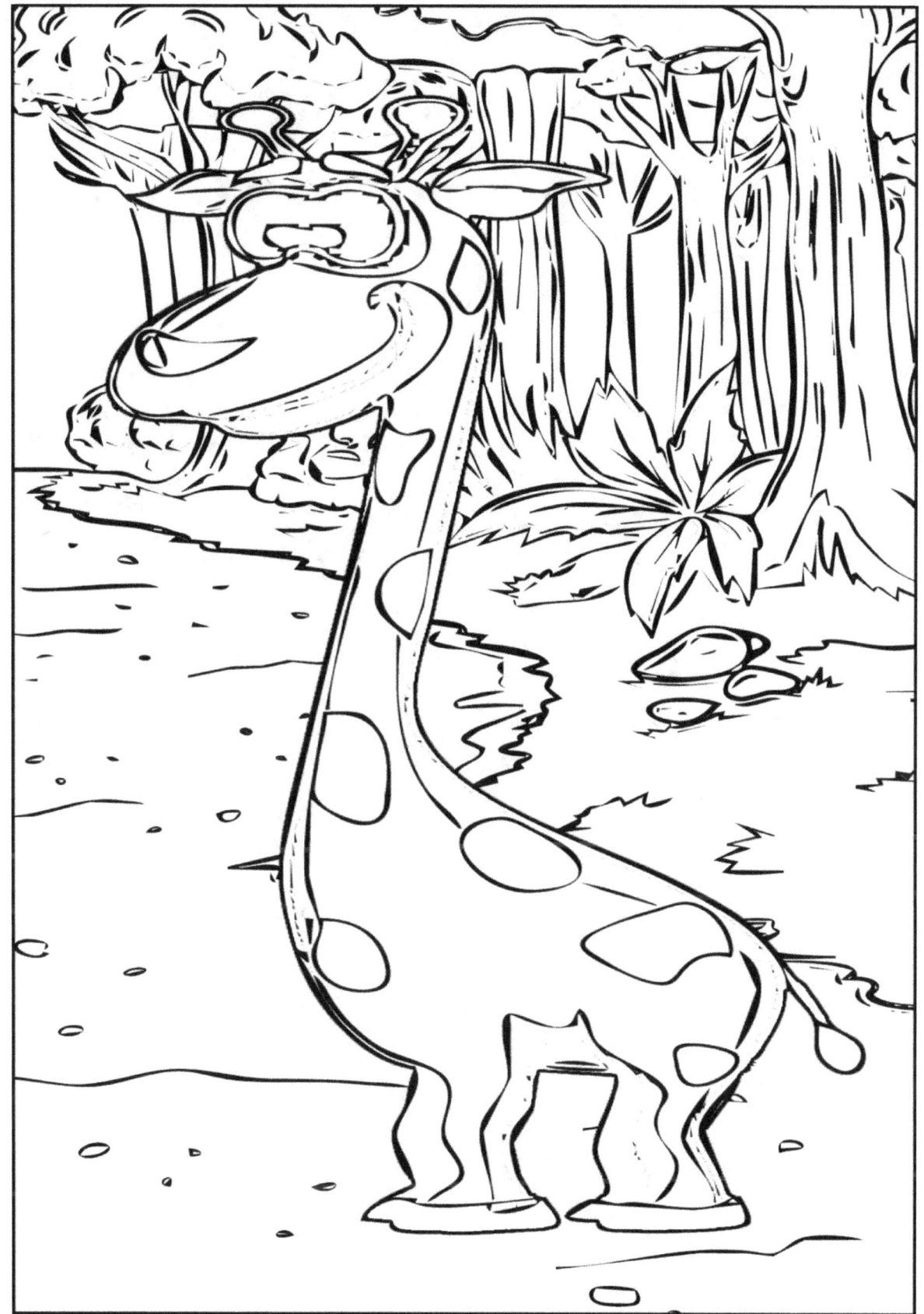

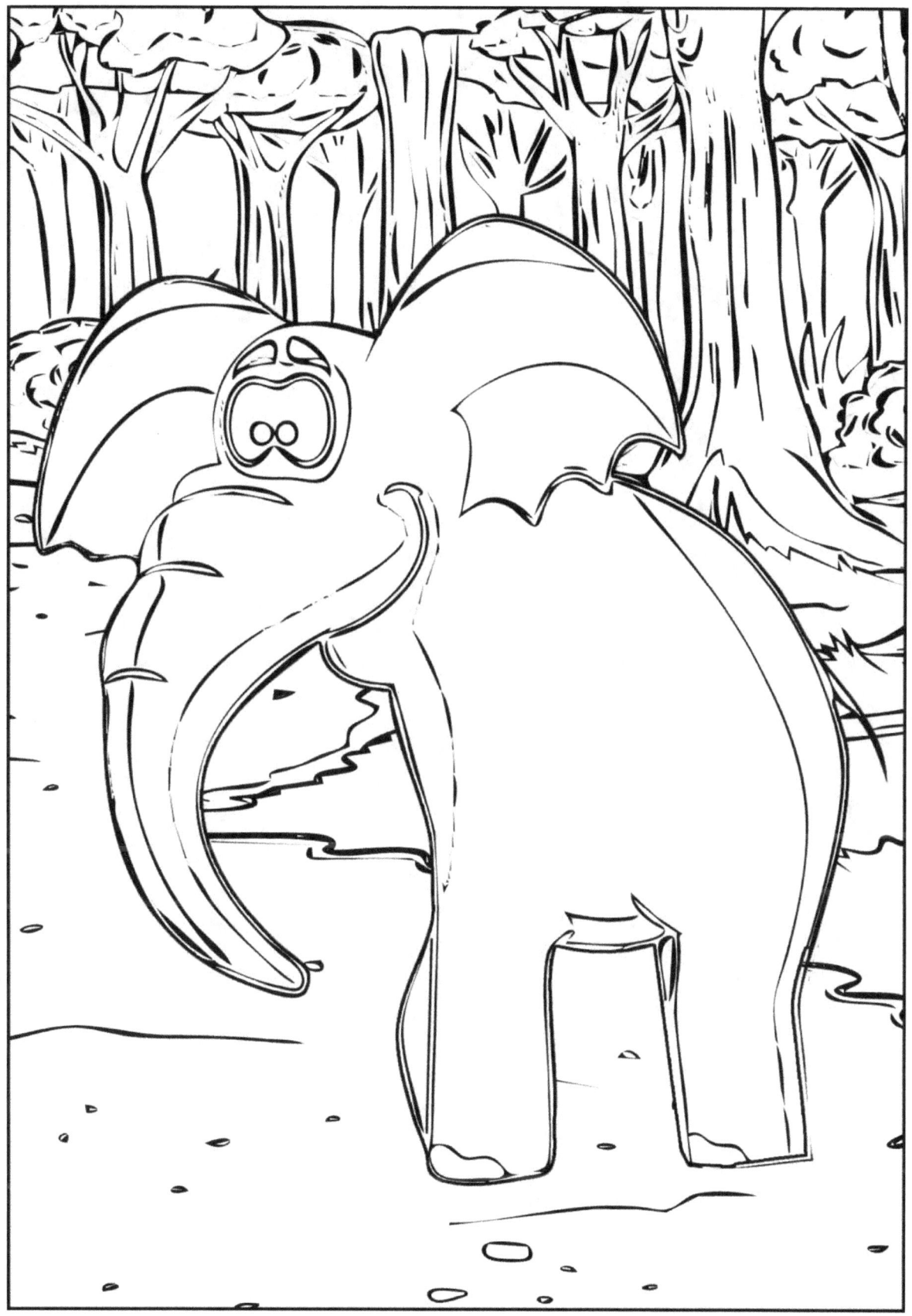

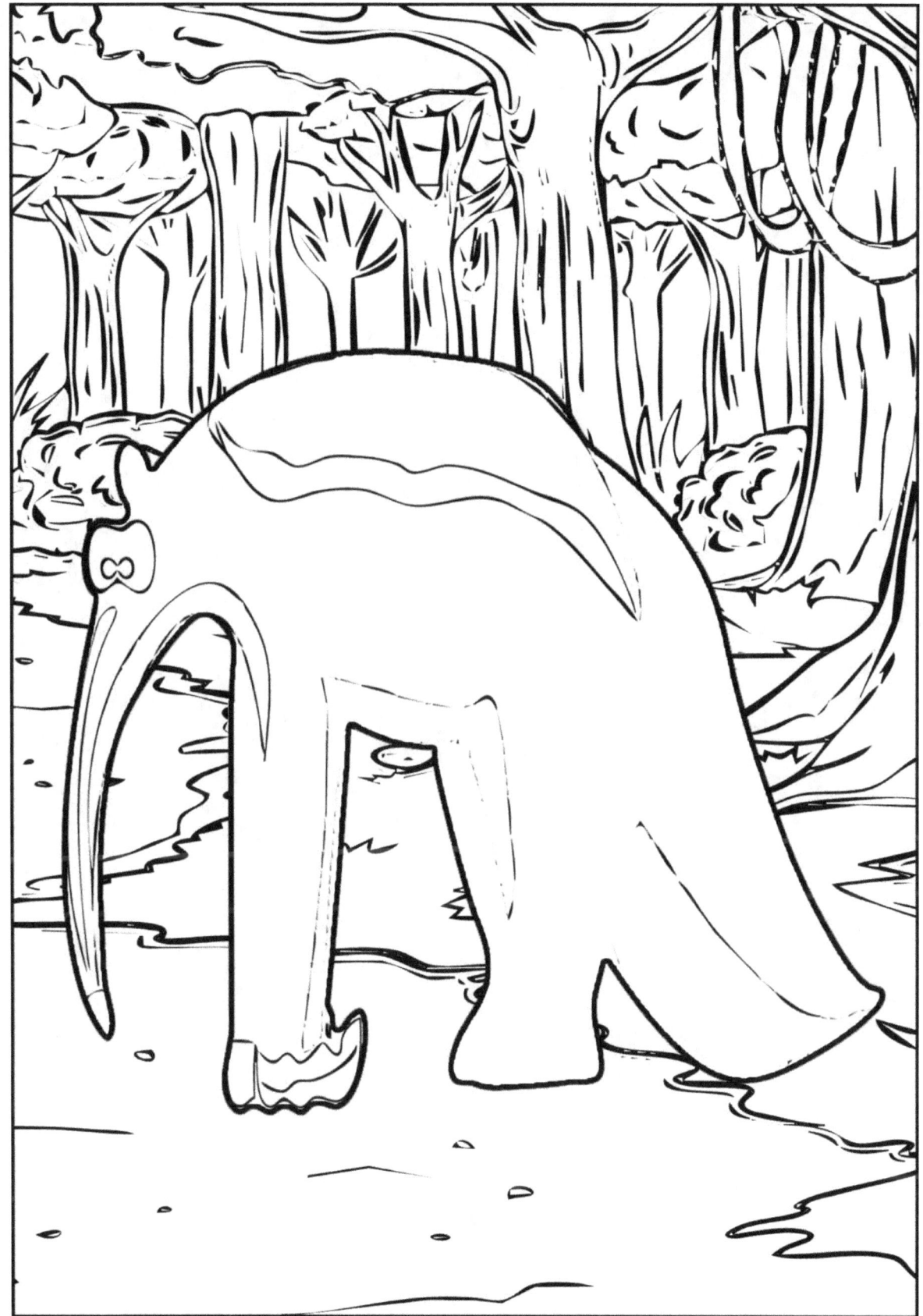

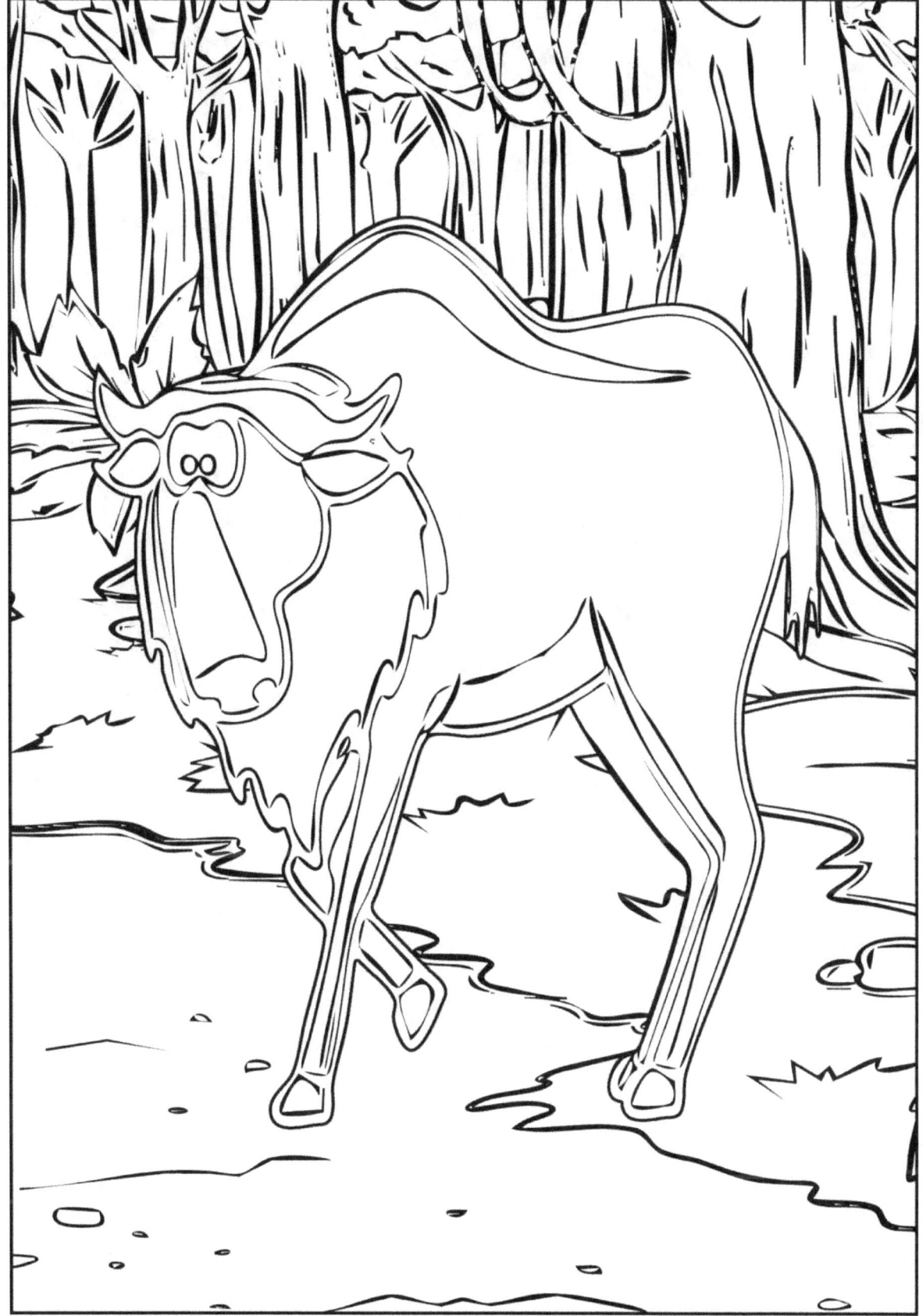

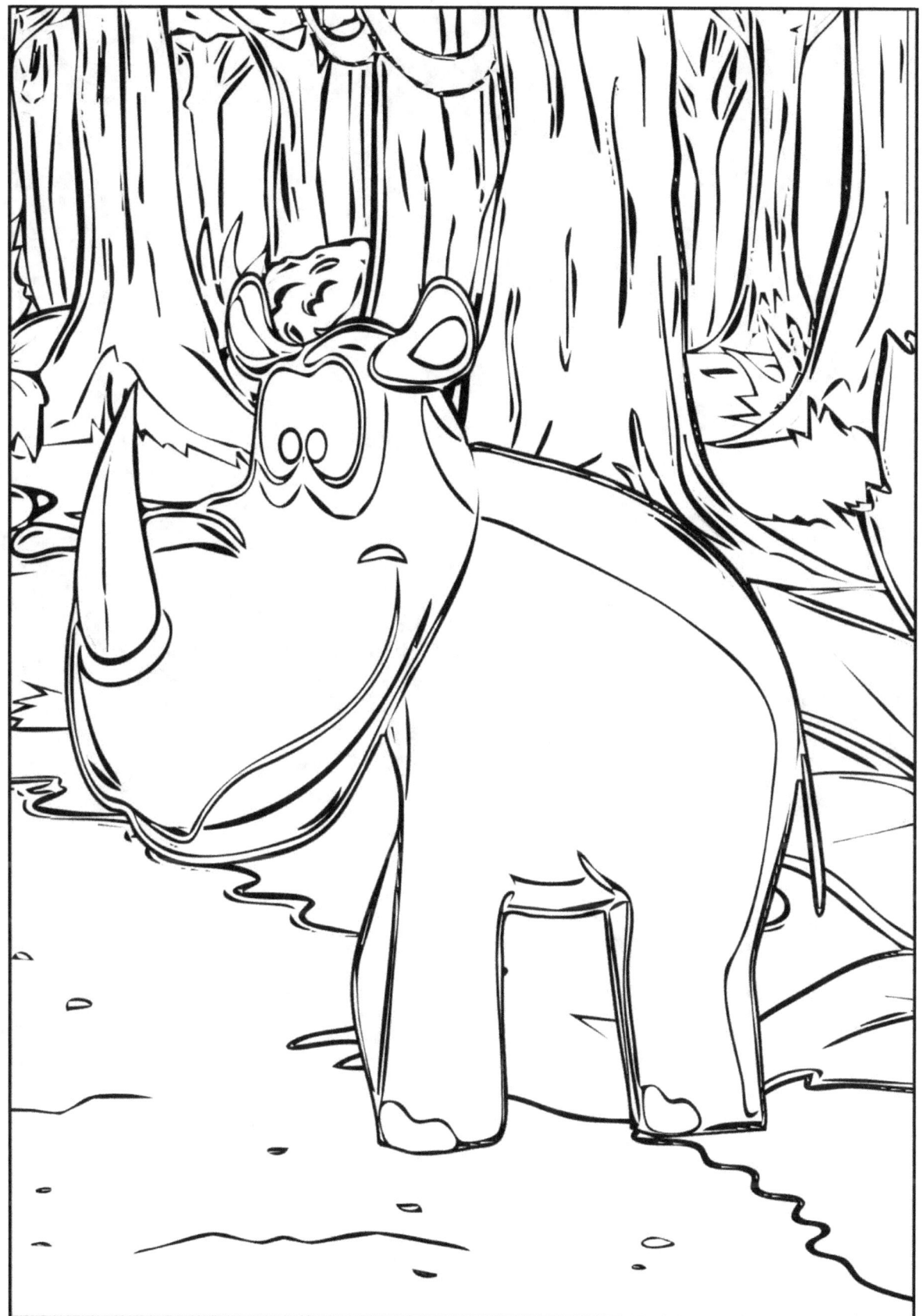

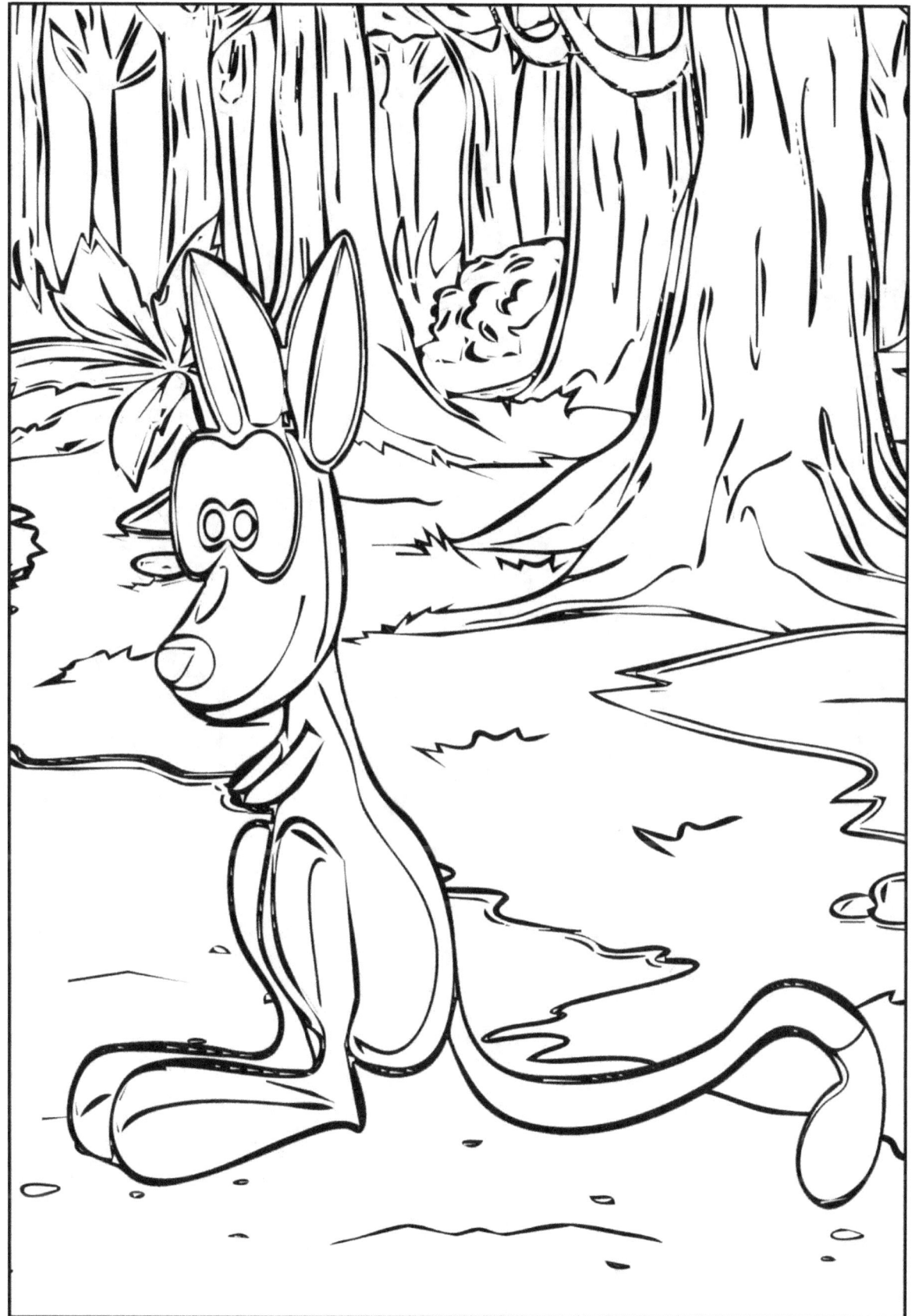

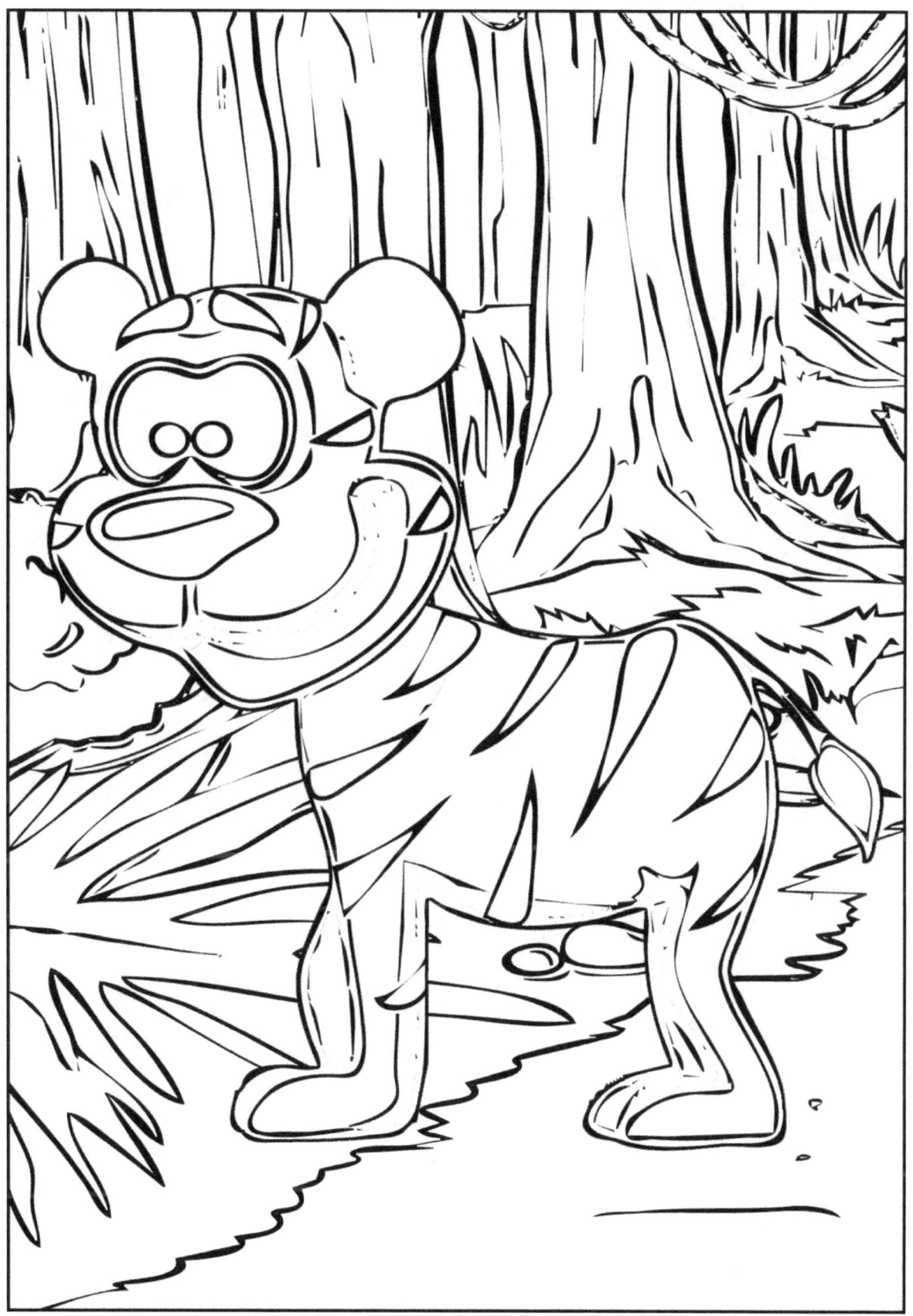

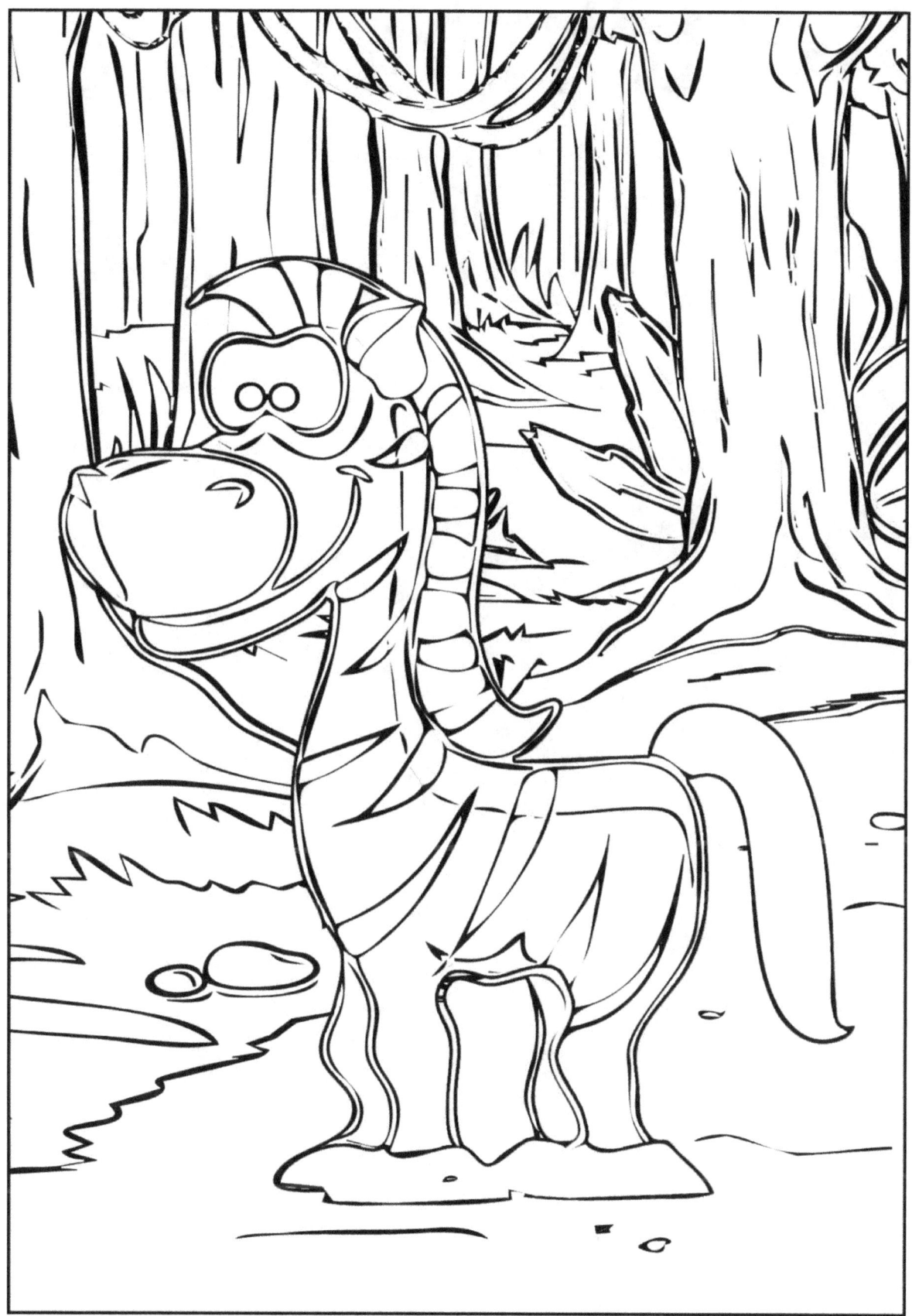

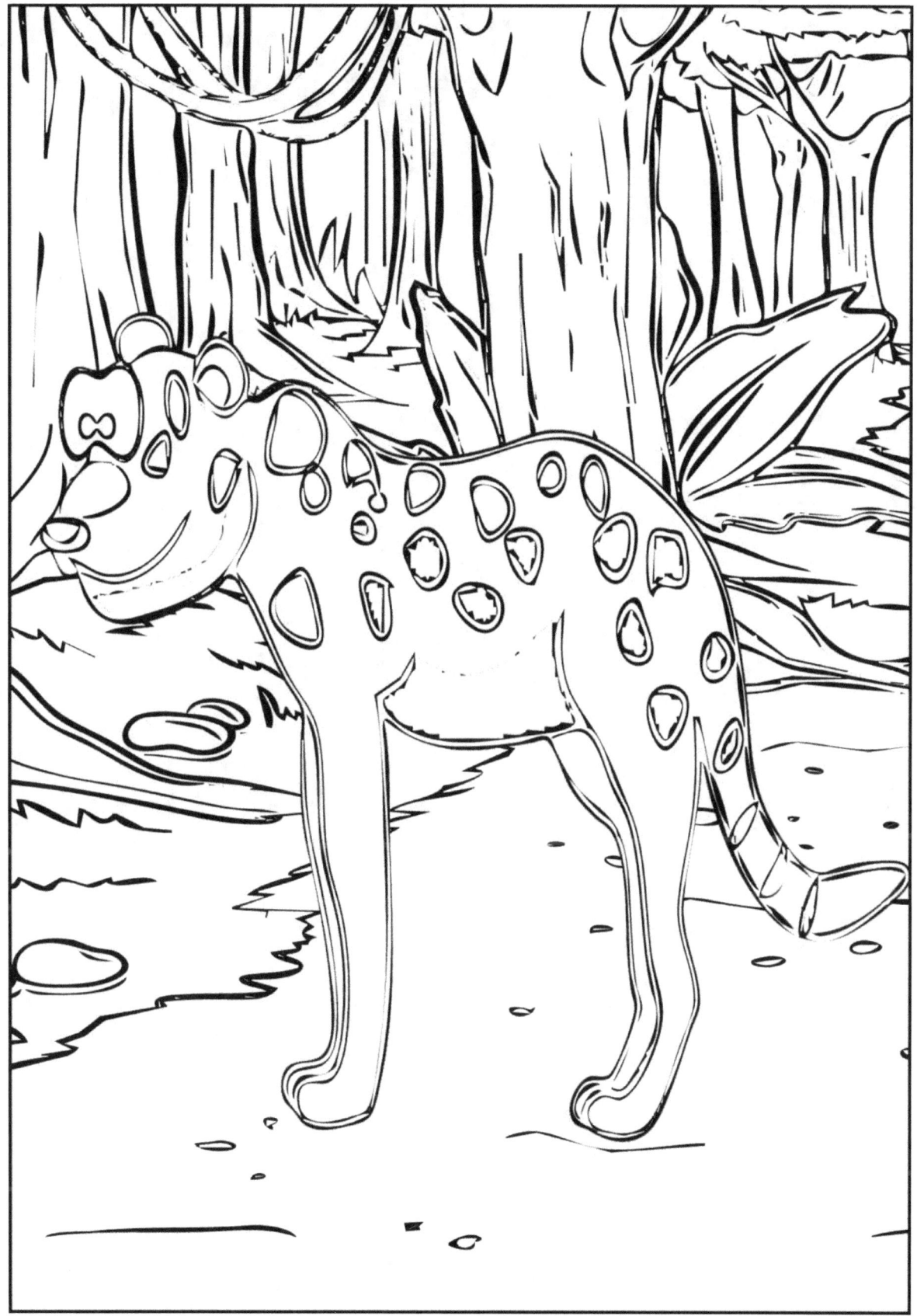

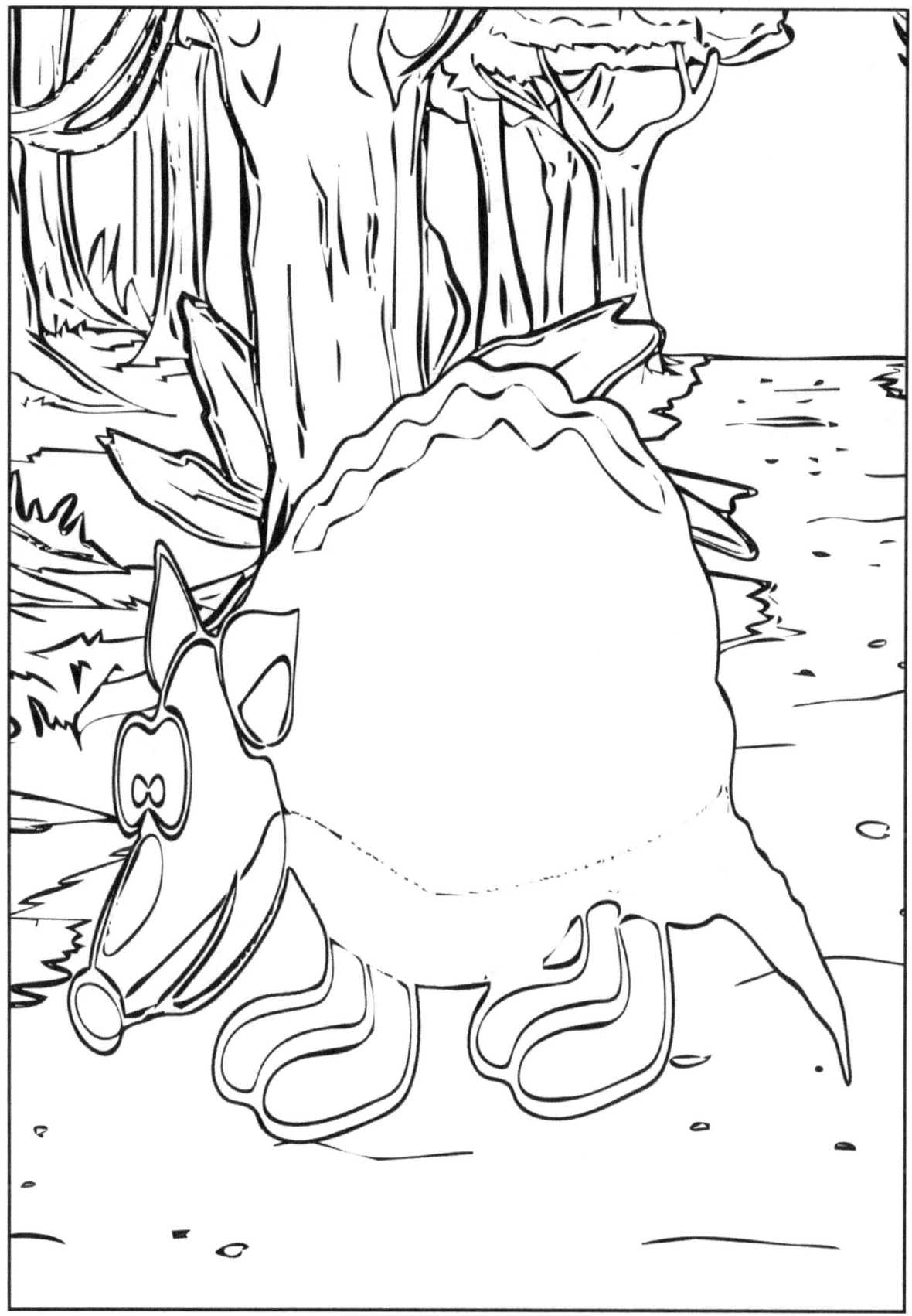

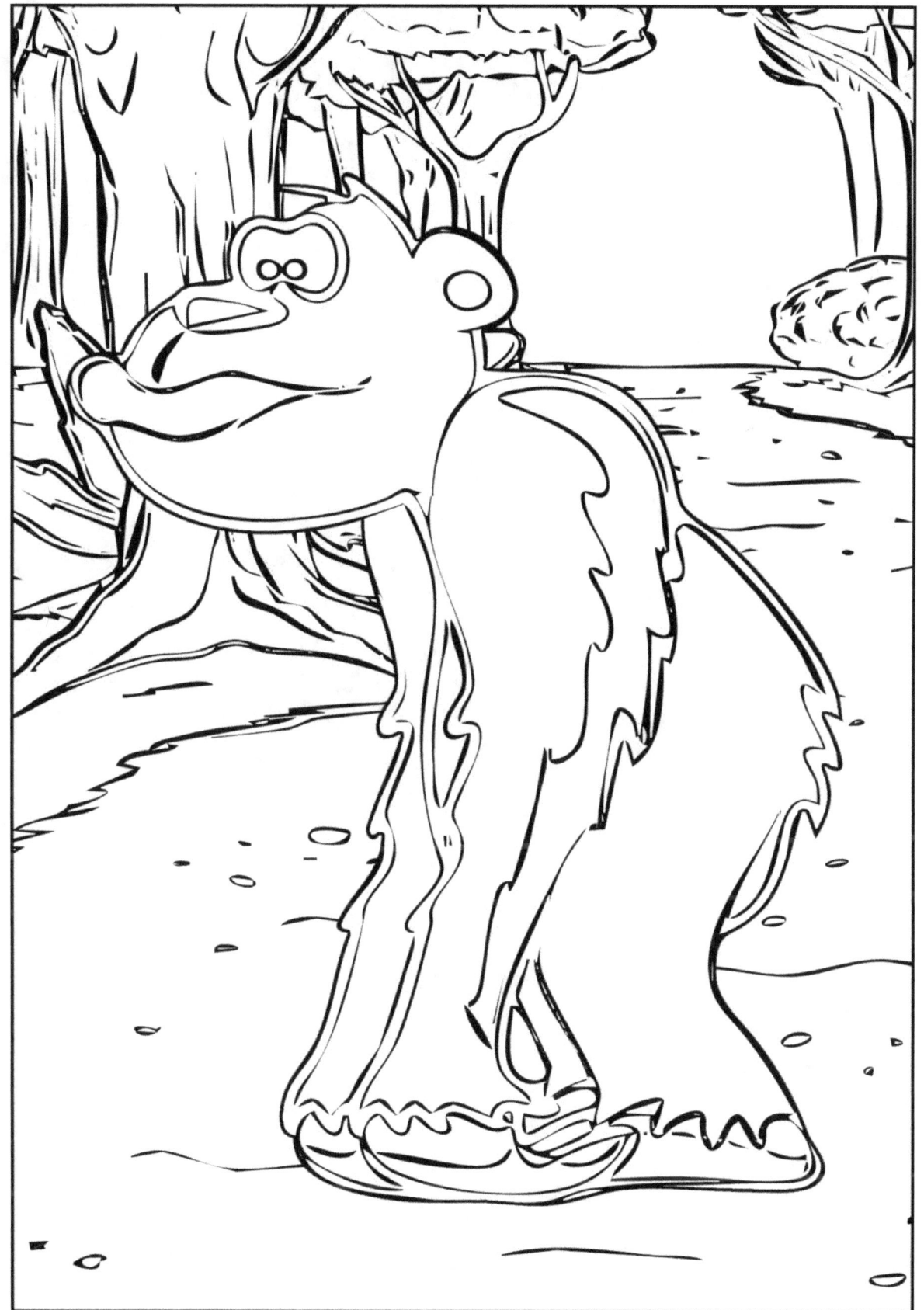

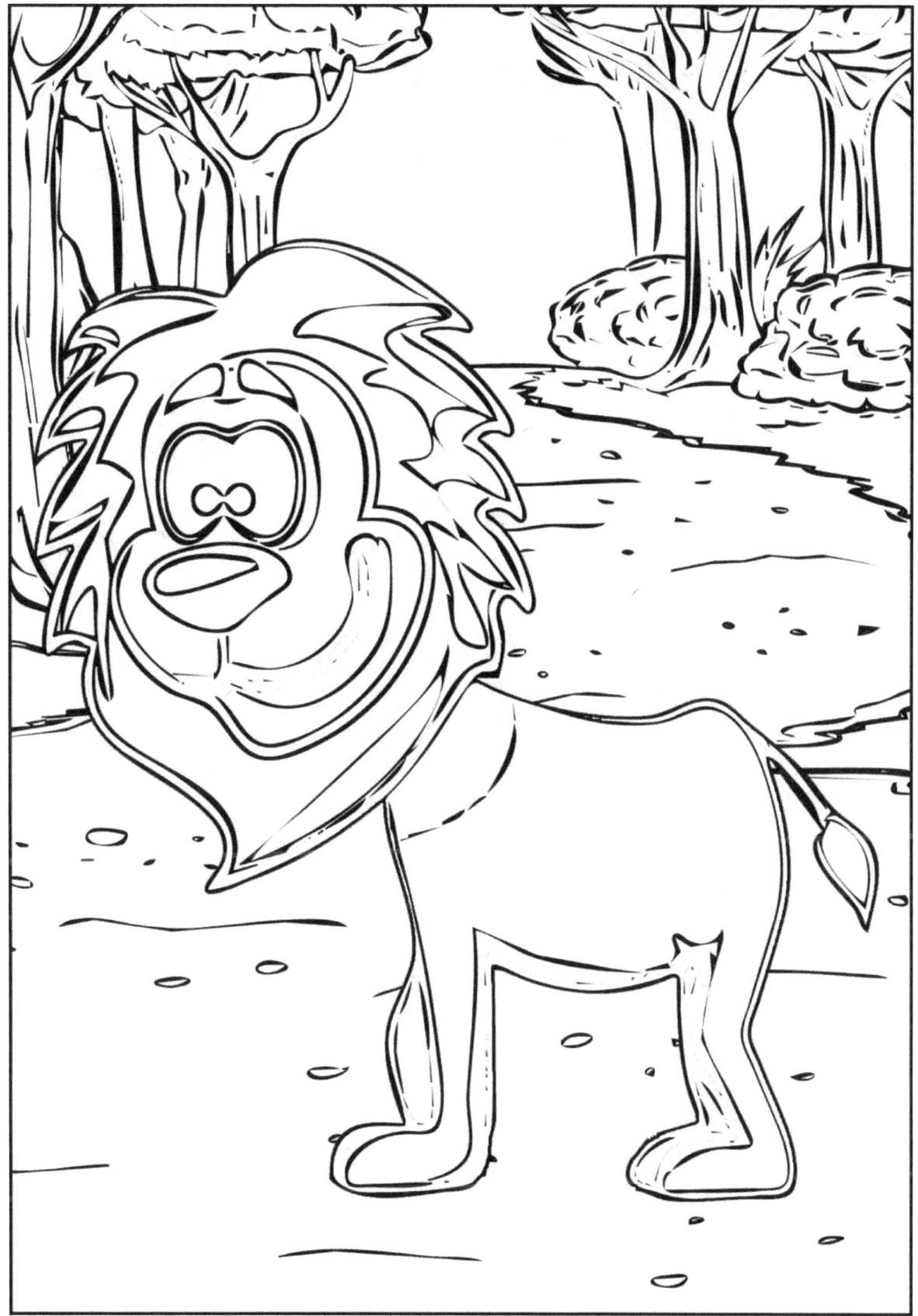

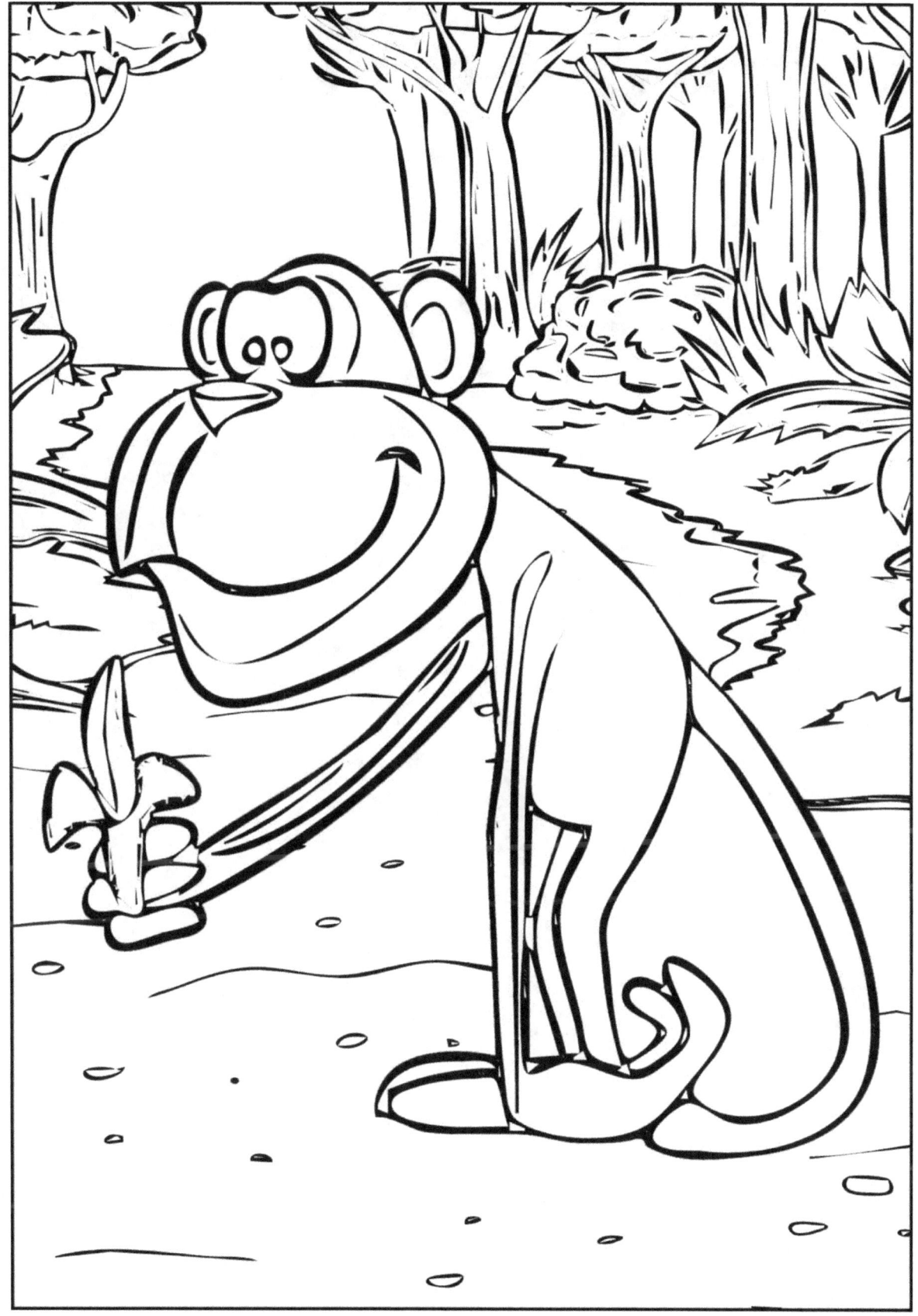

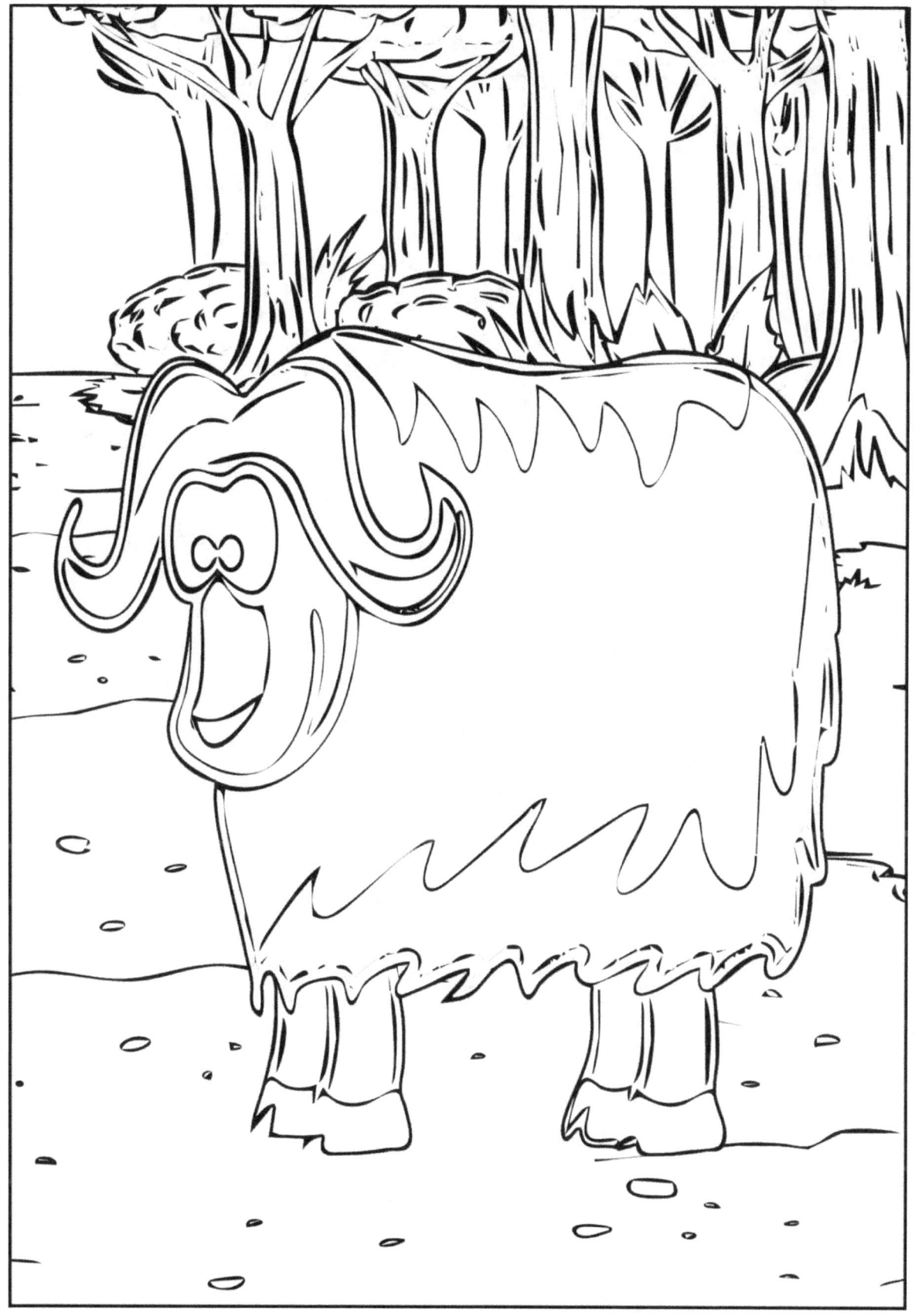

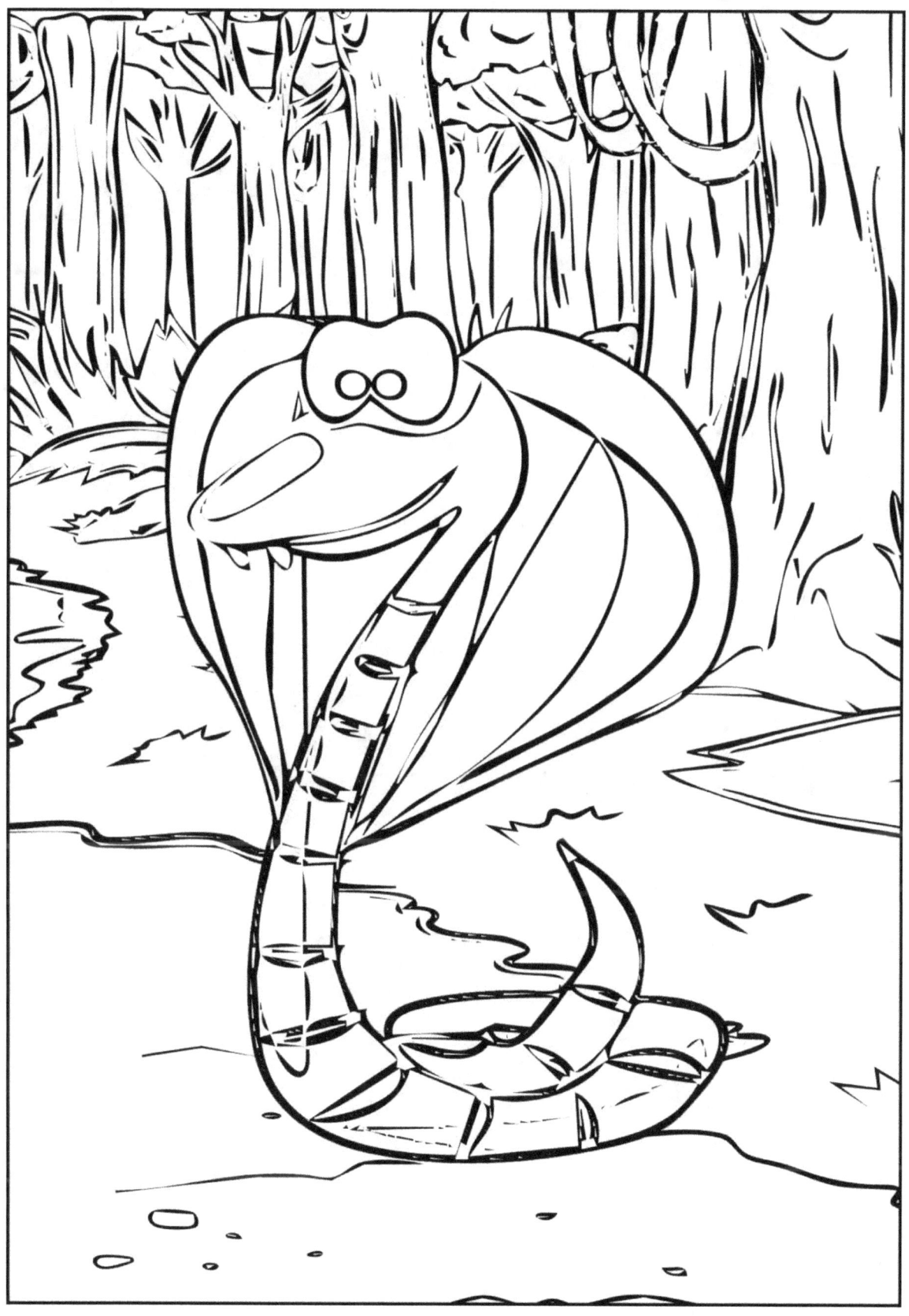

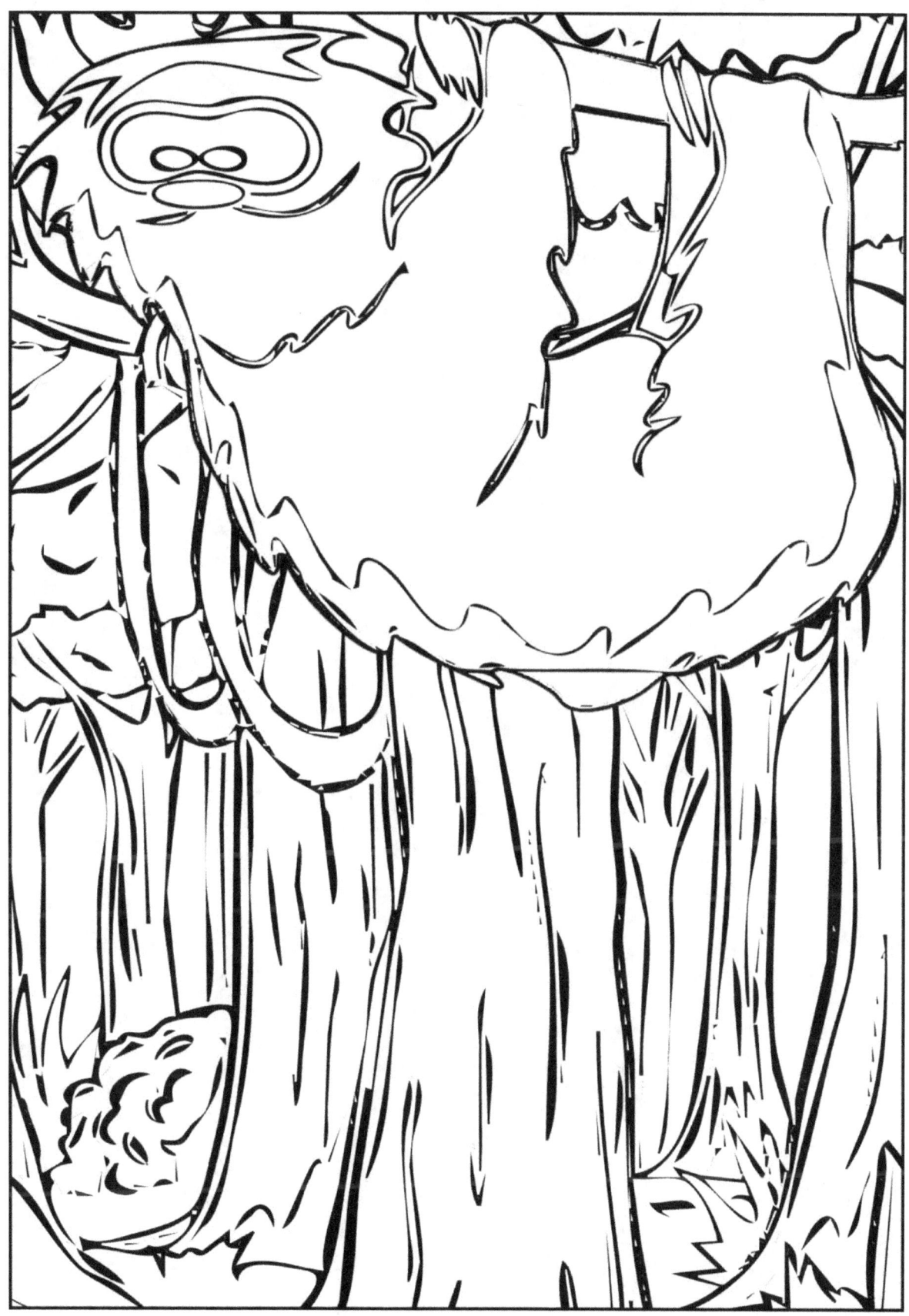

ANIMALS

Doing Very Human Things

Coloring Book

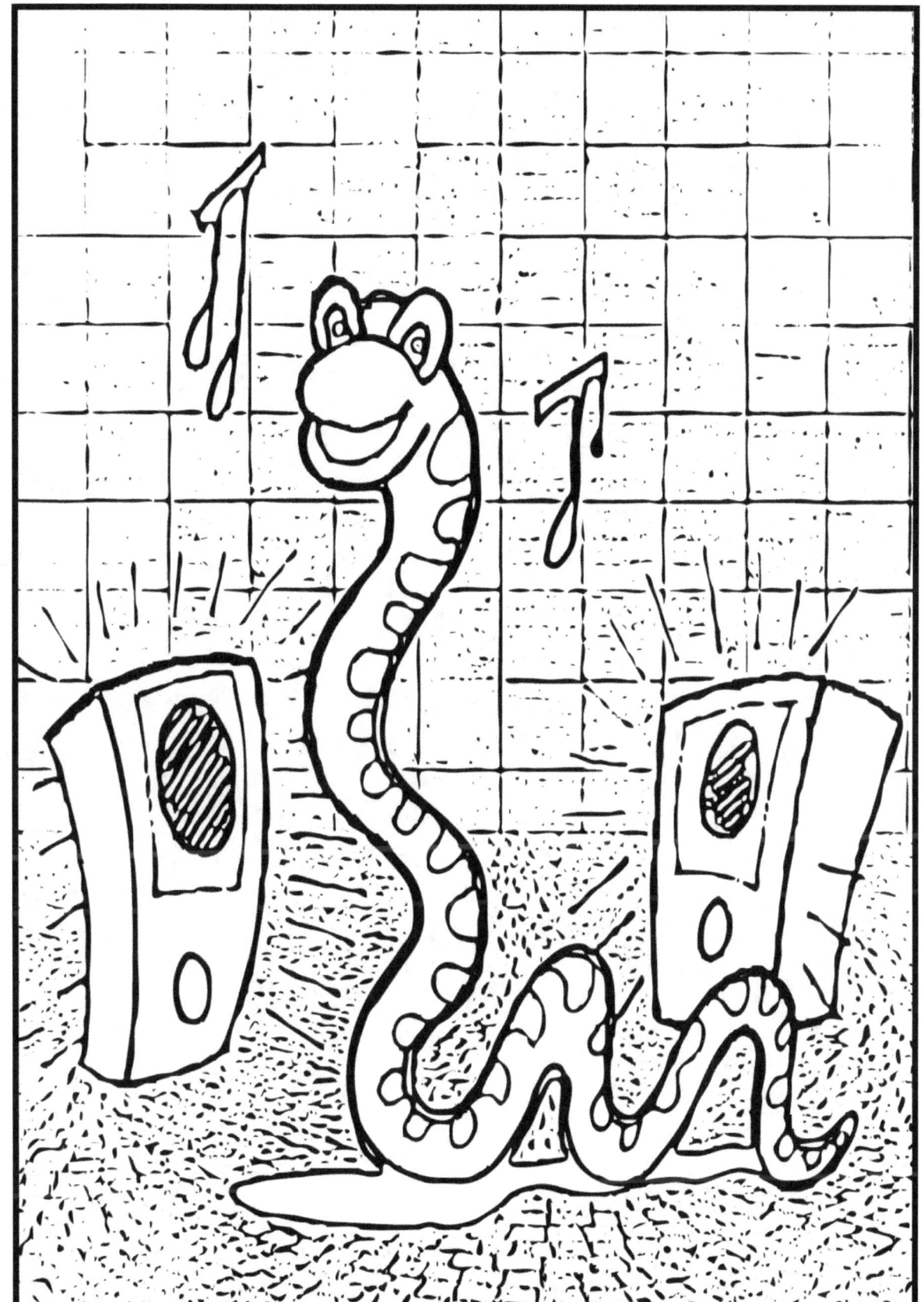

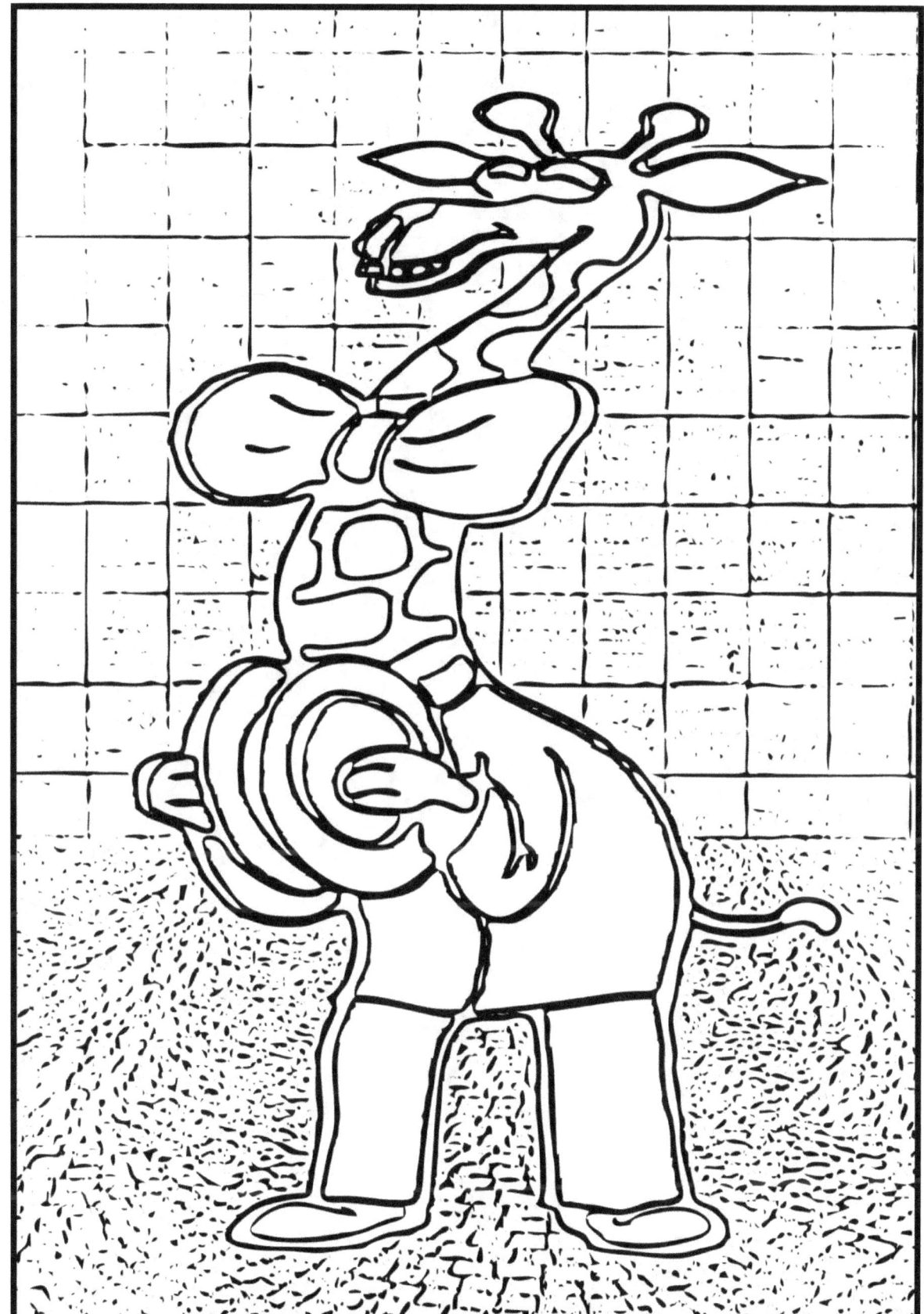

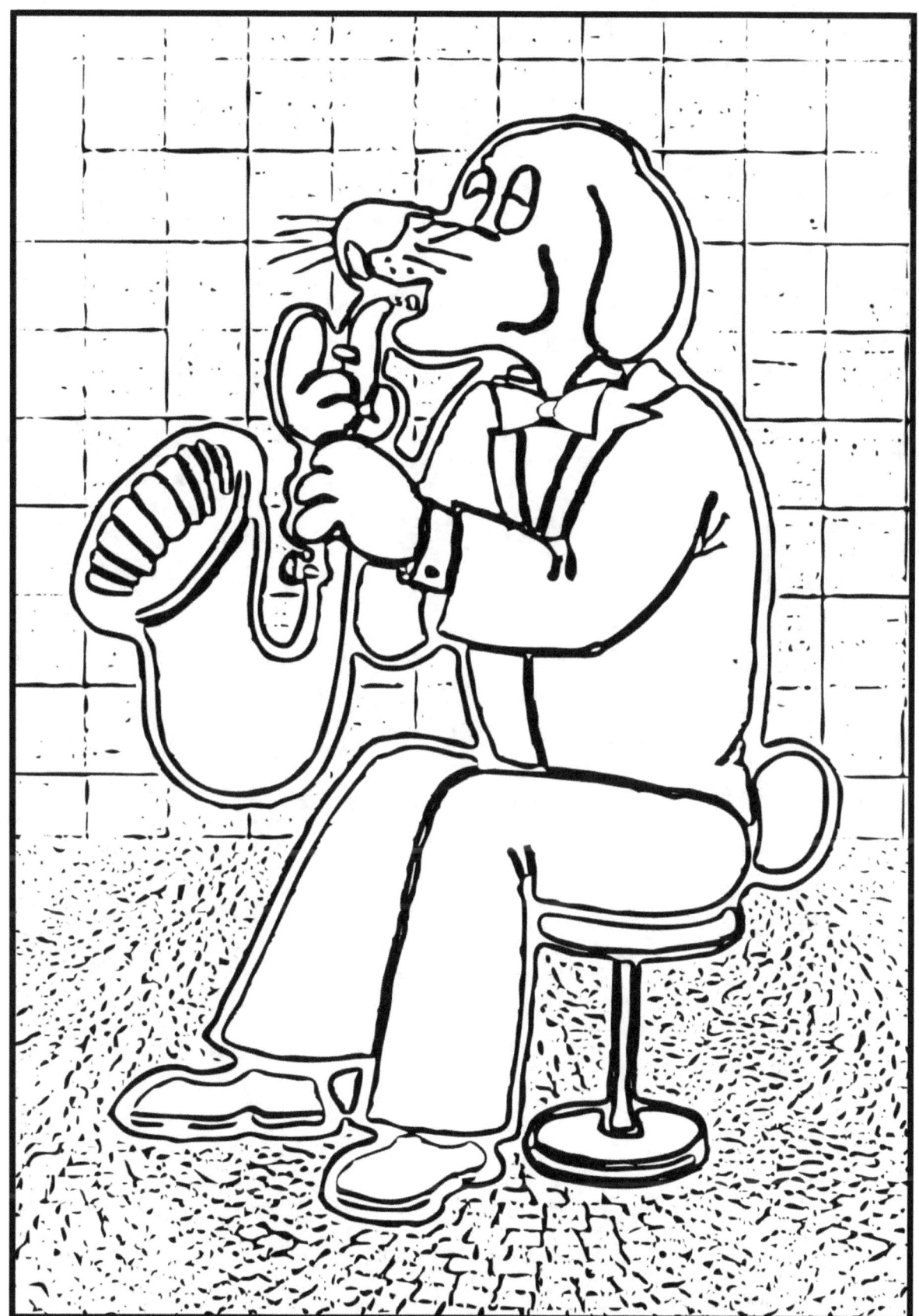

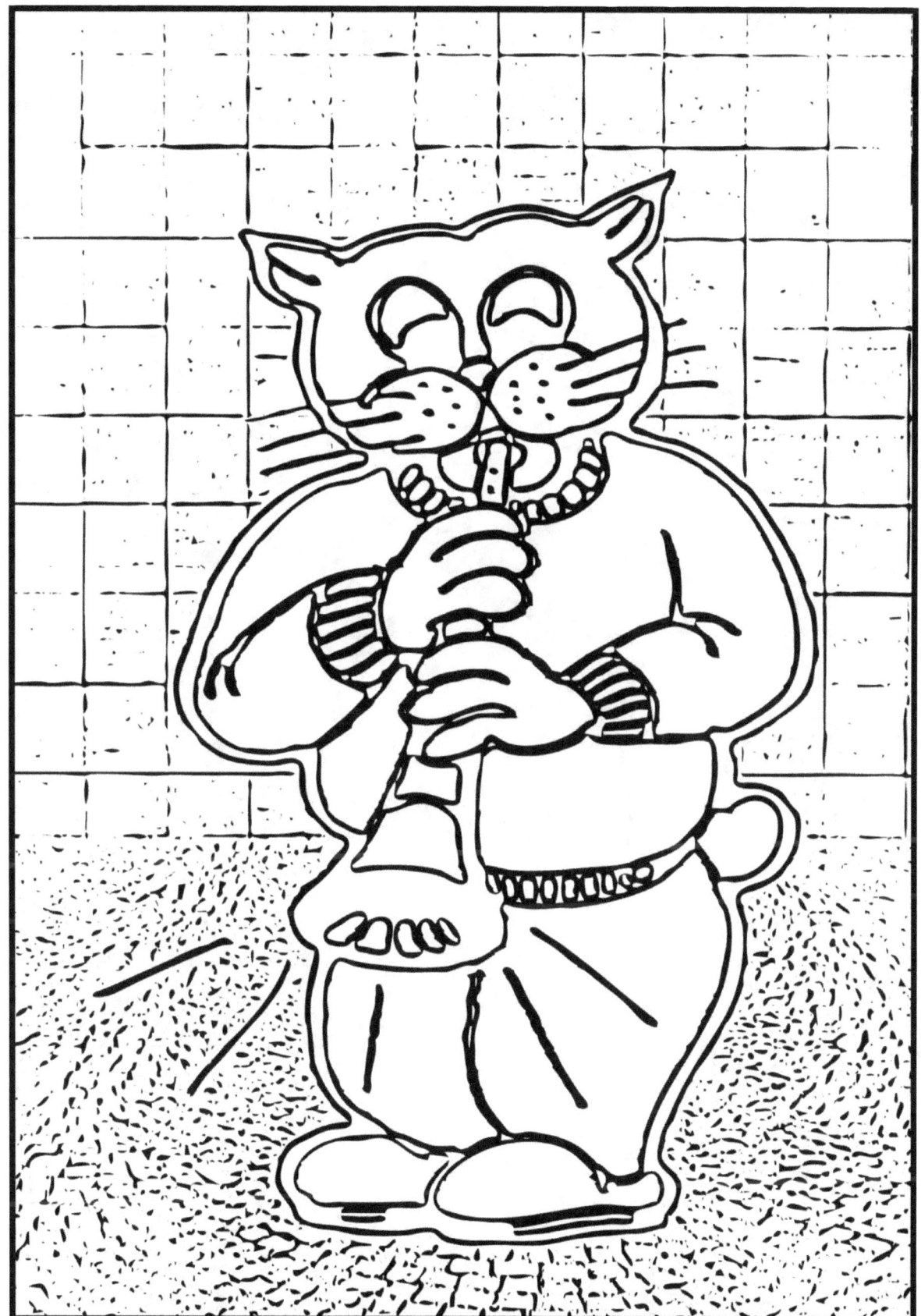

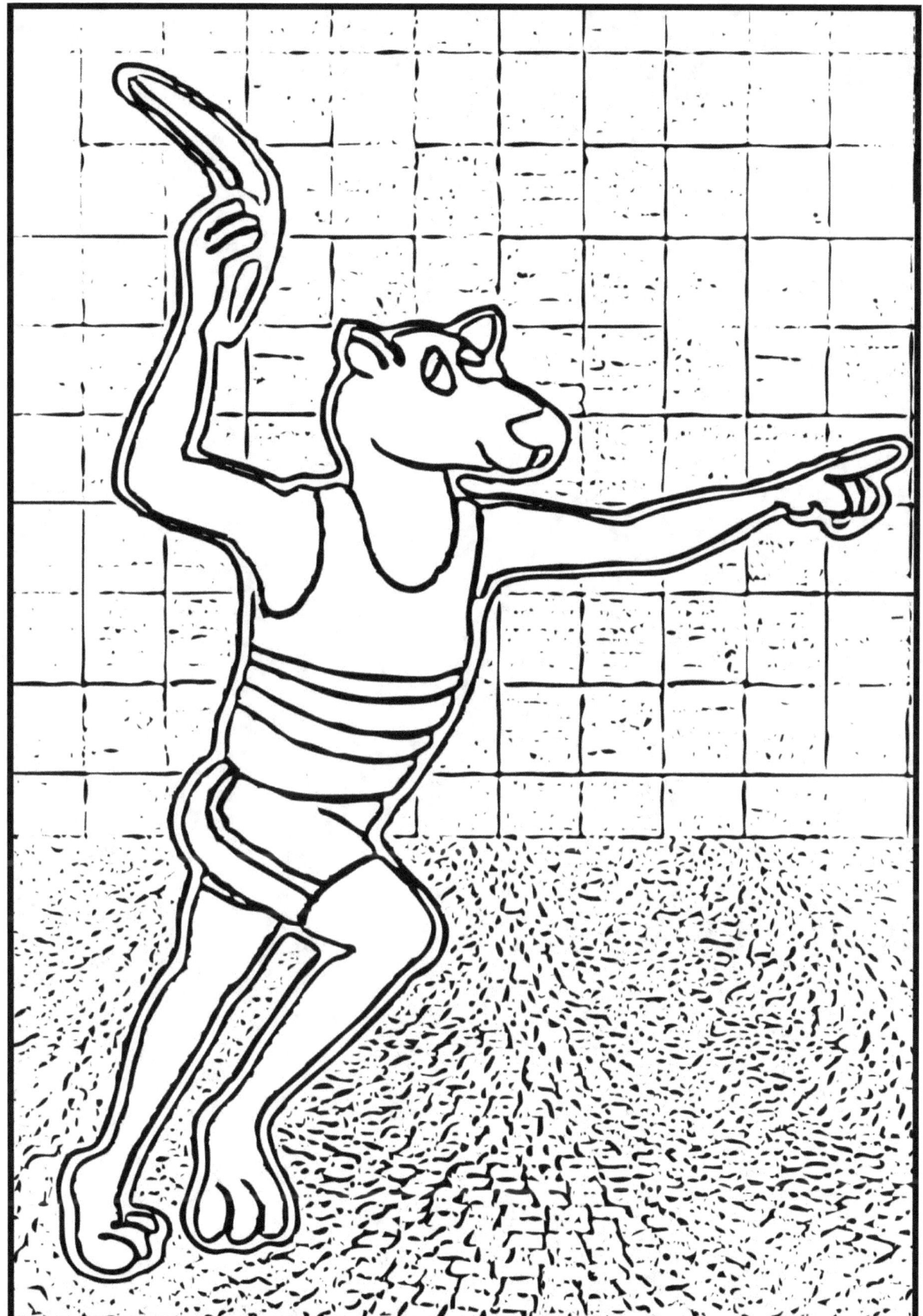

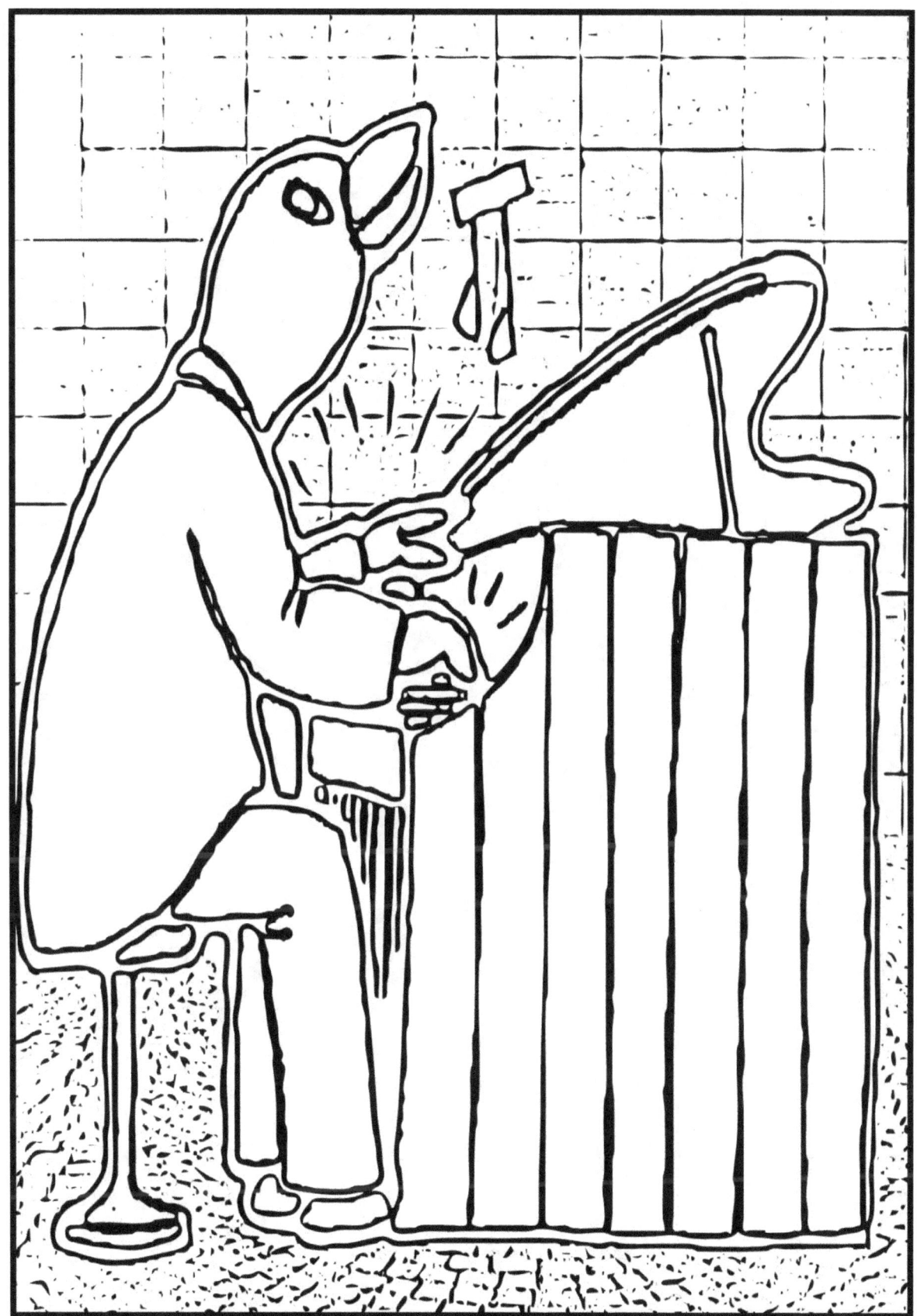

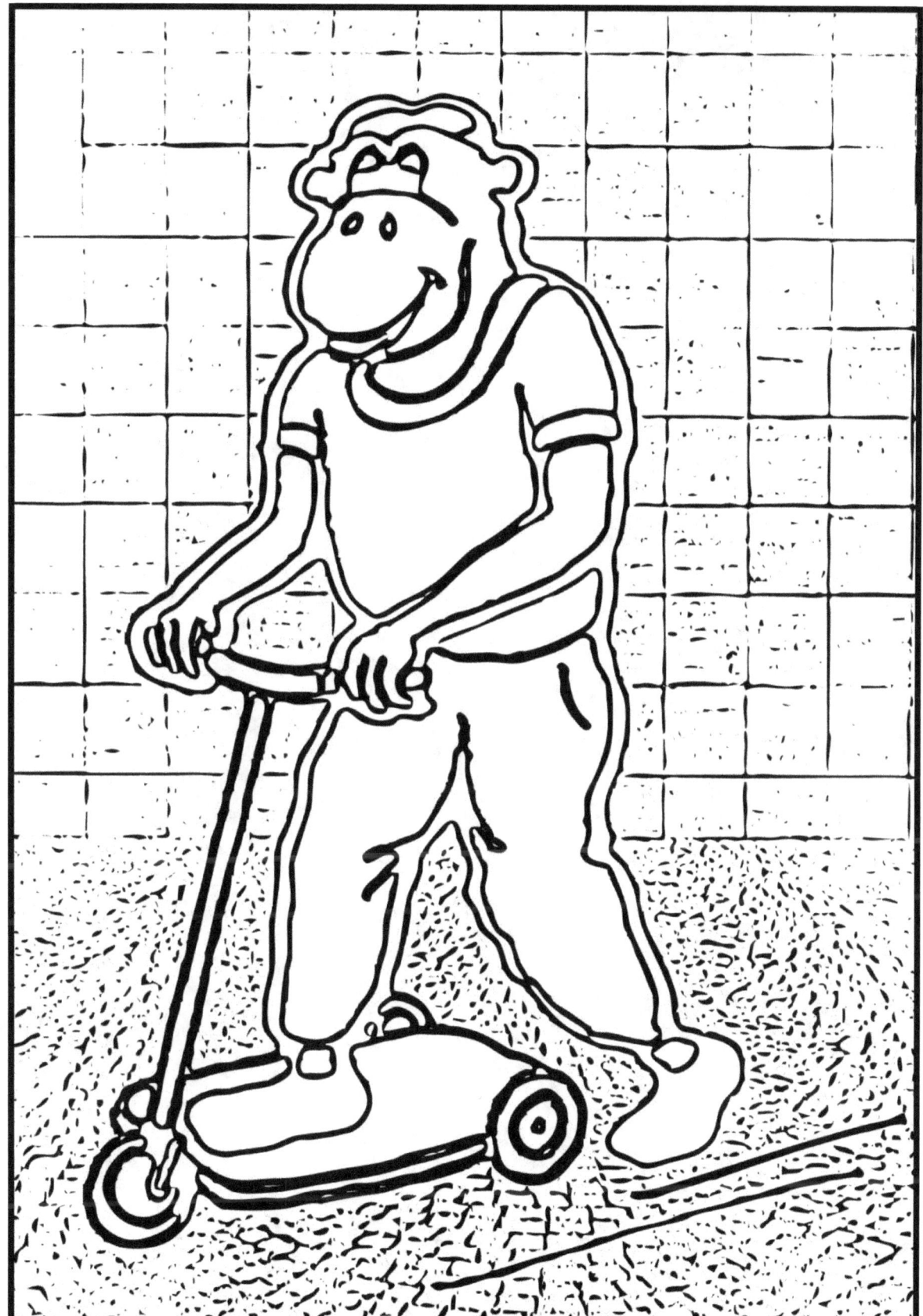

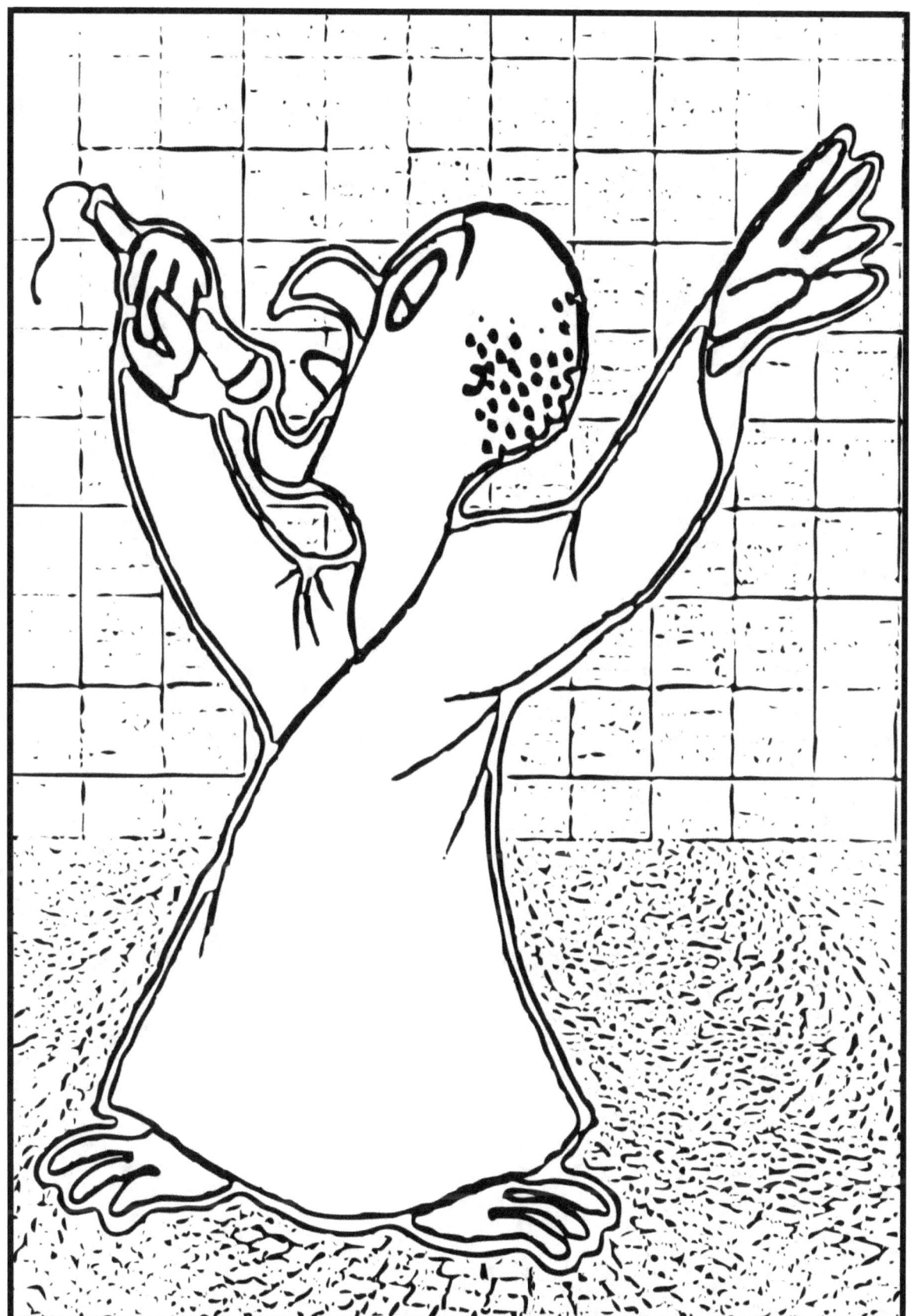

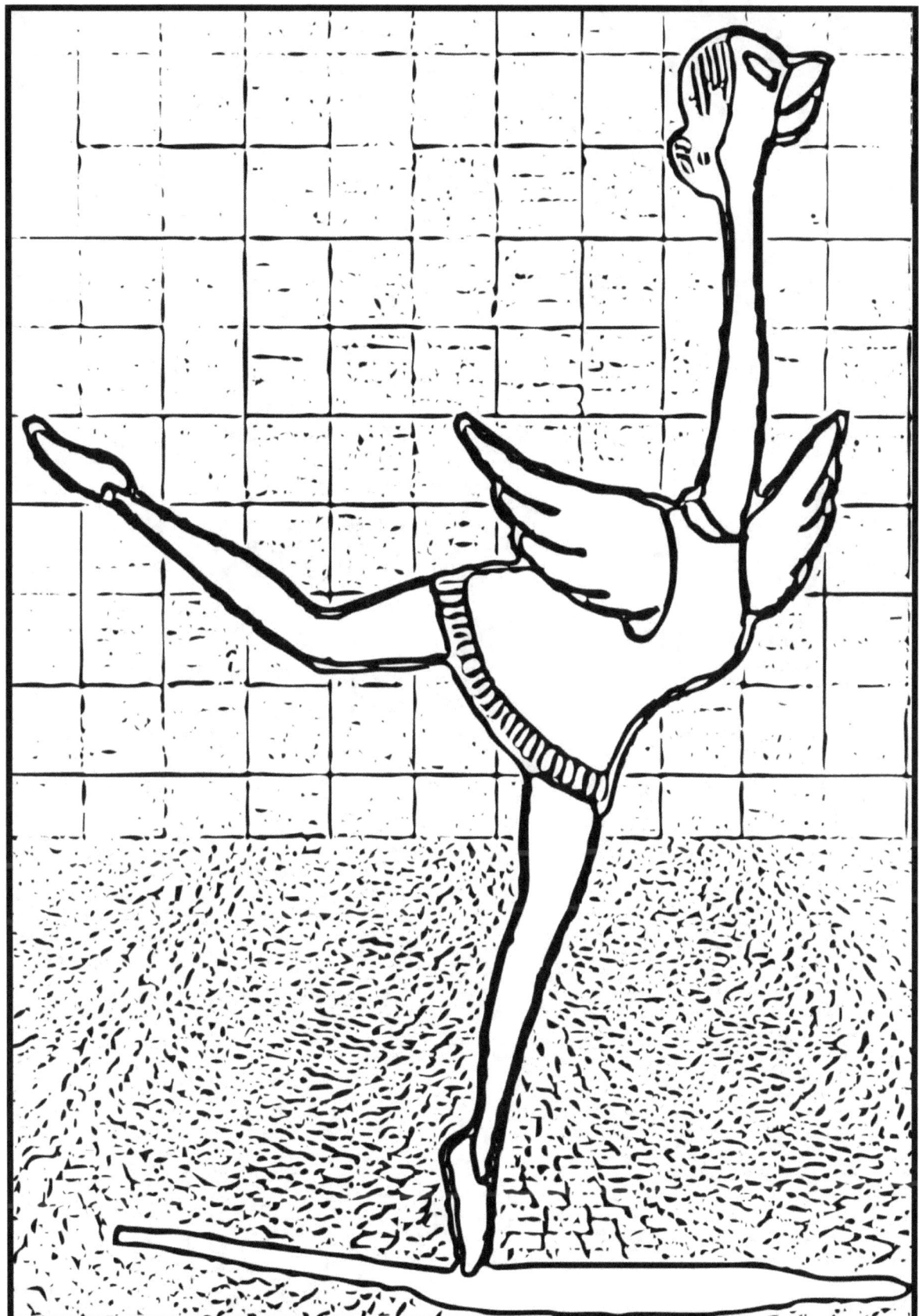

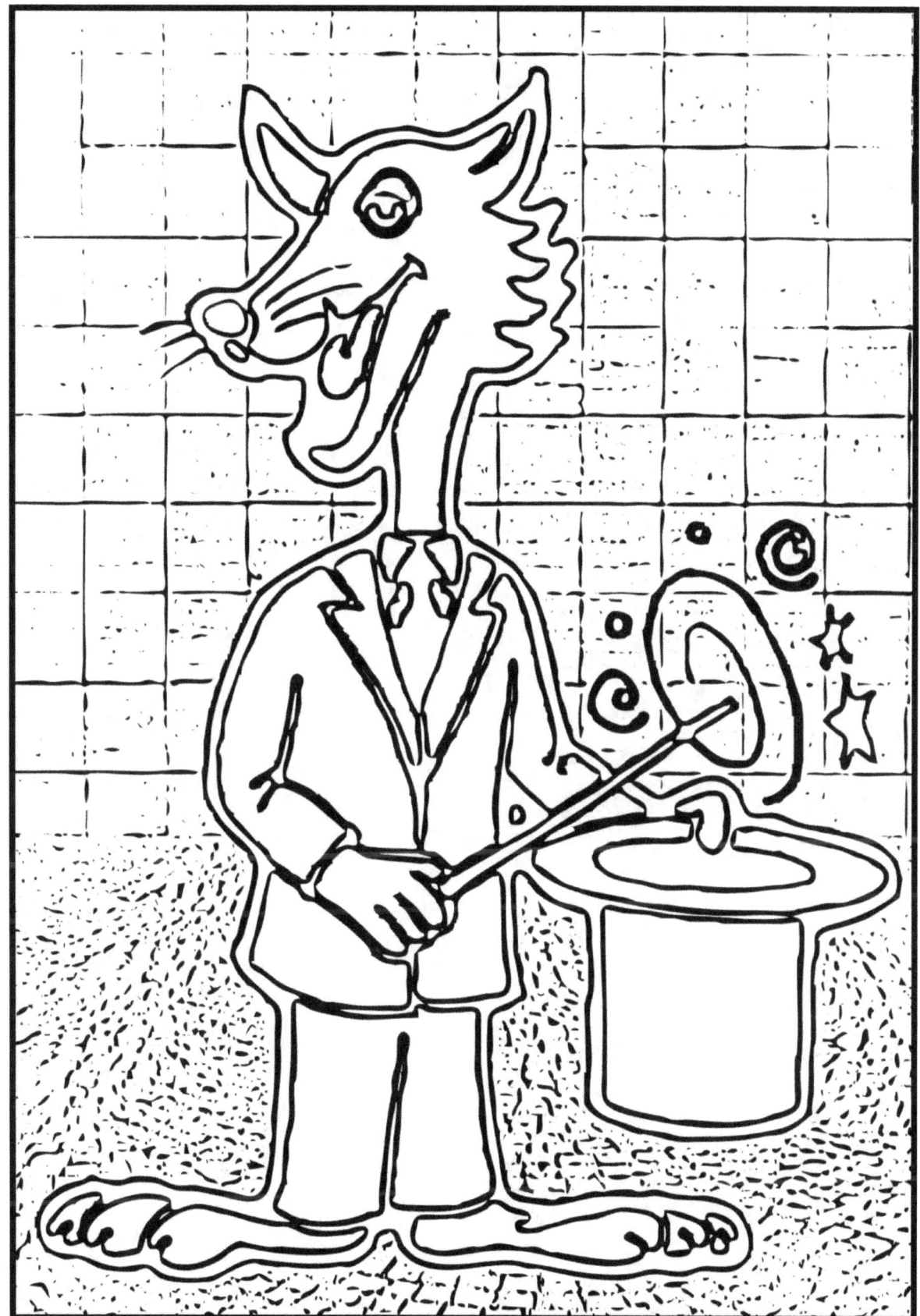

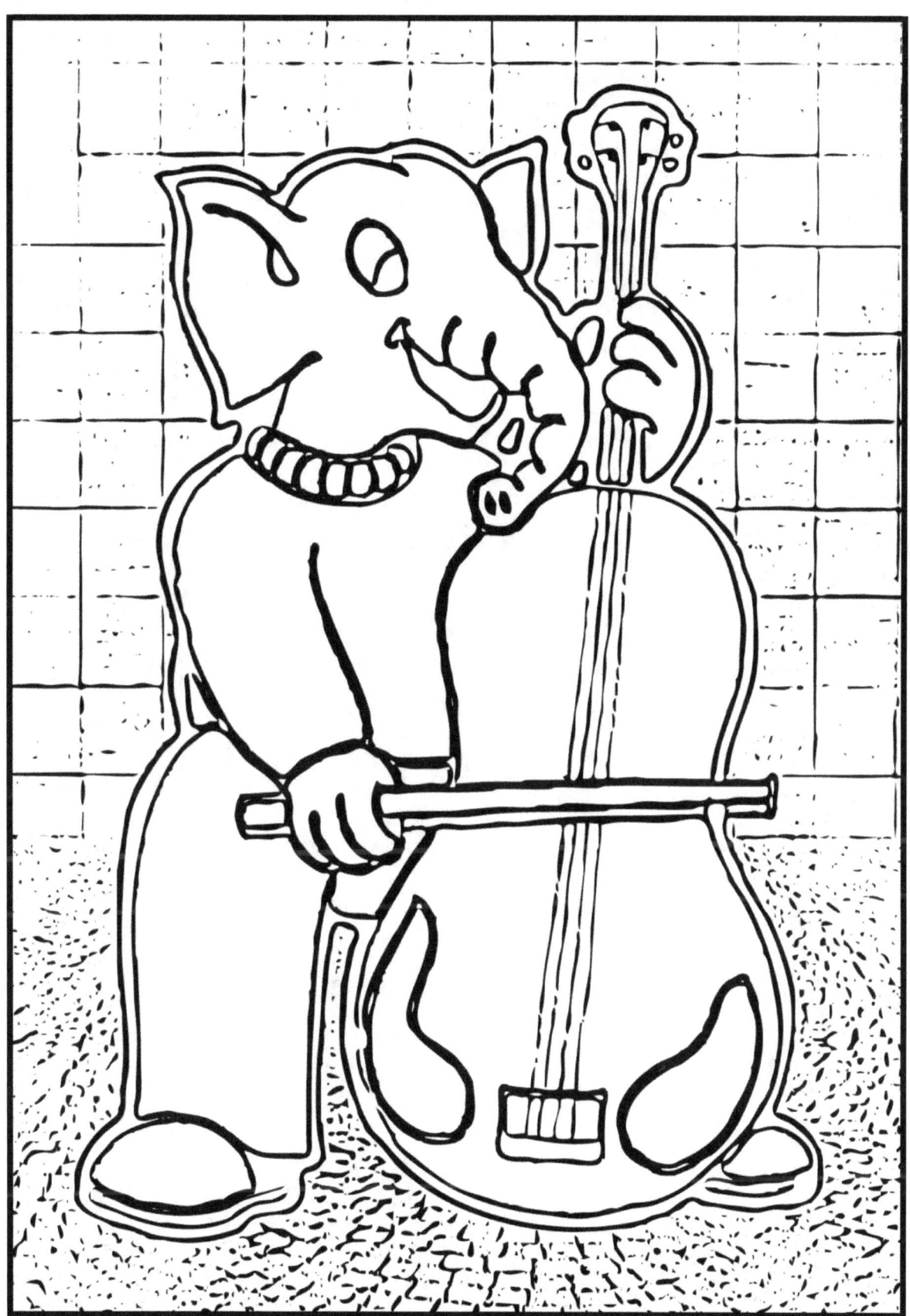

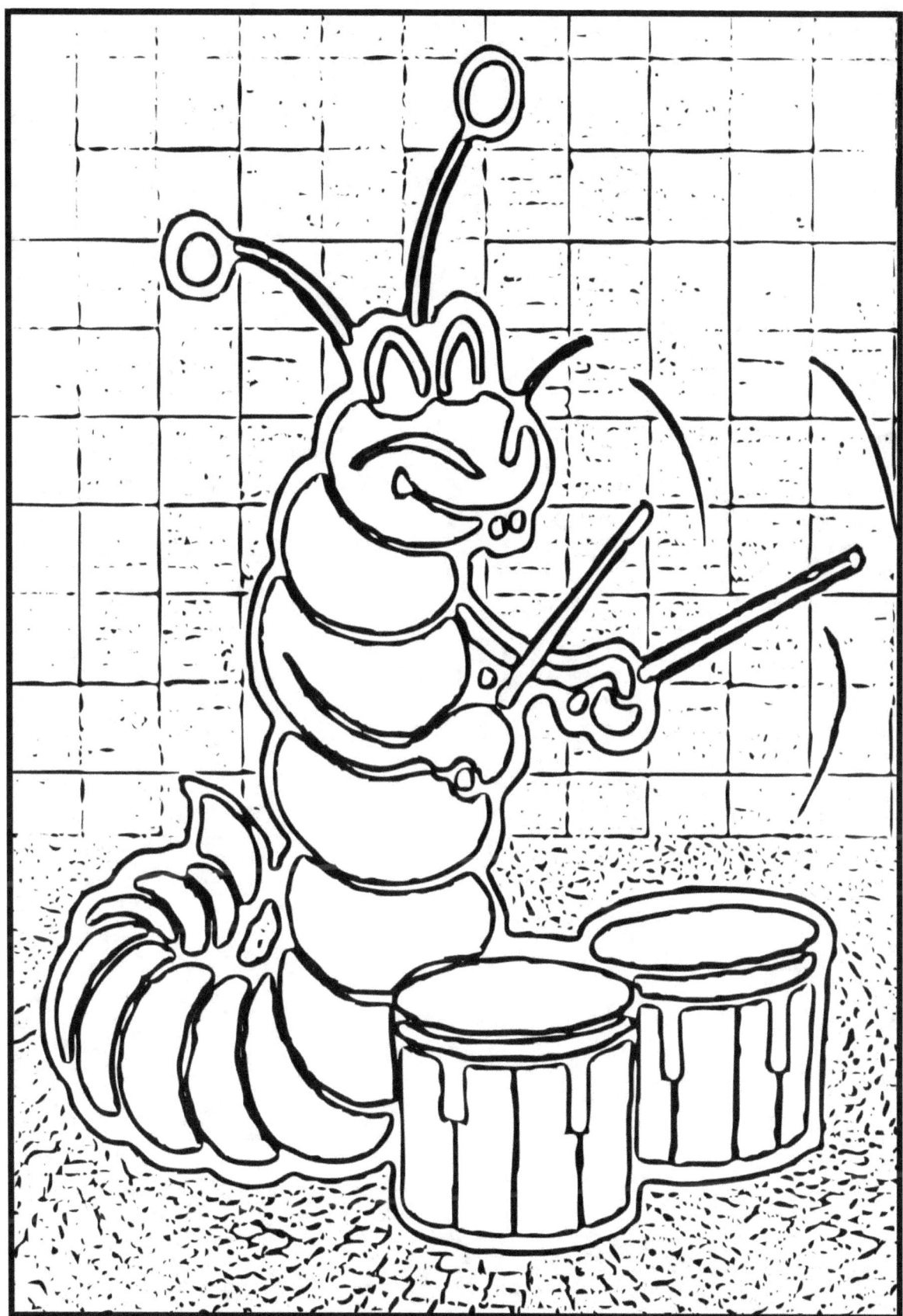

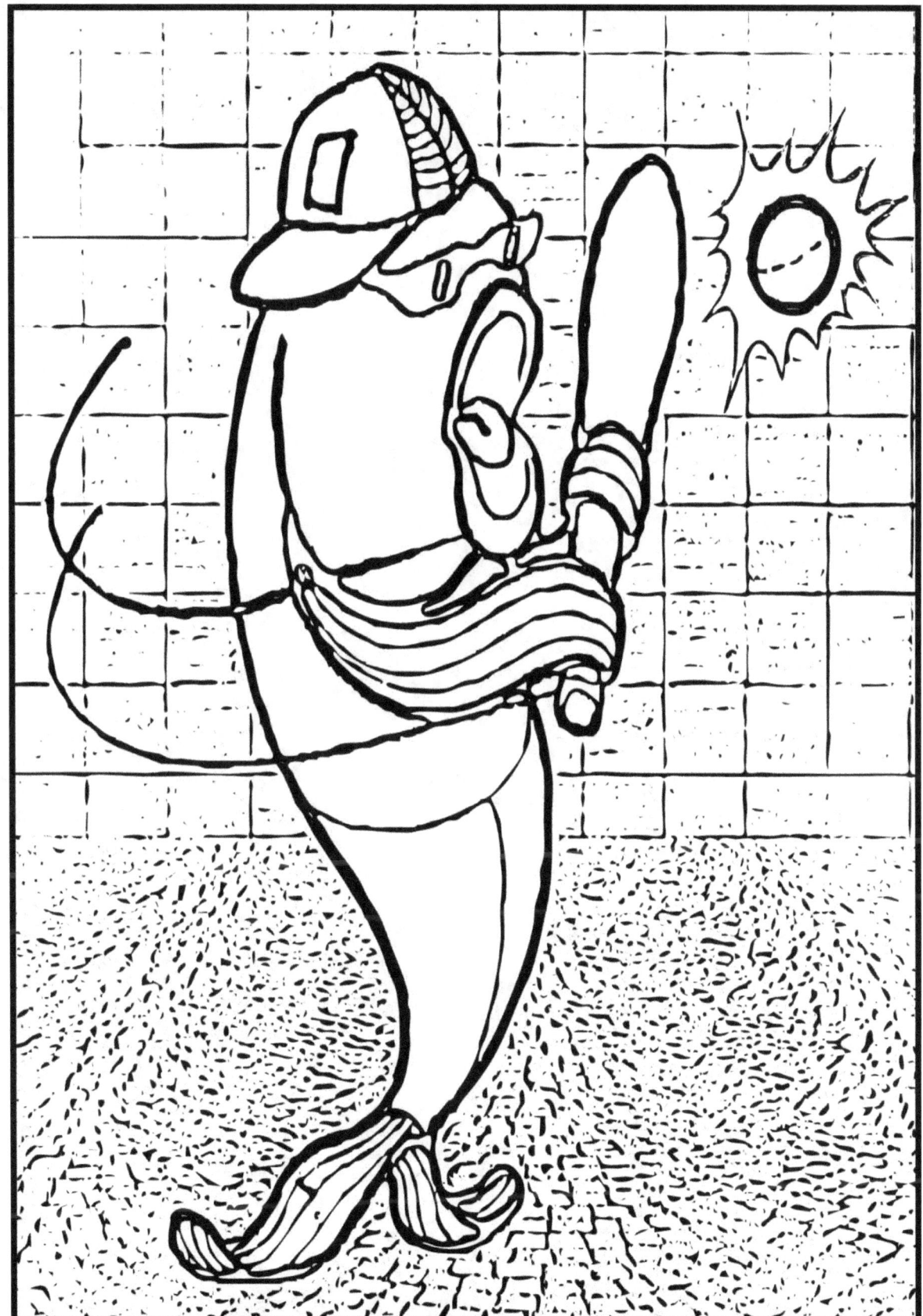

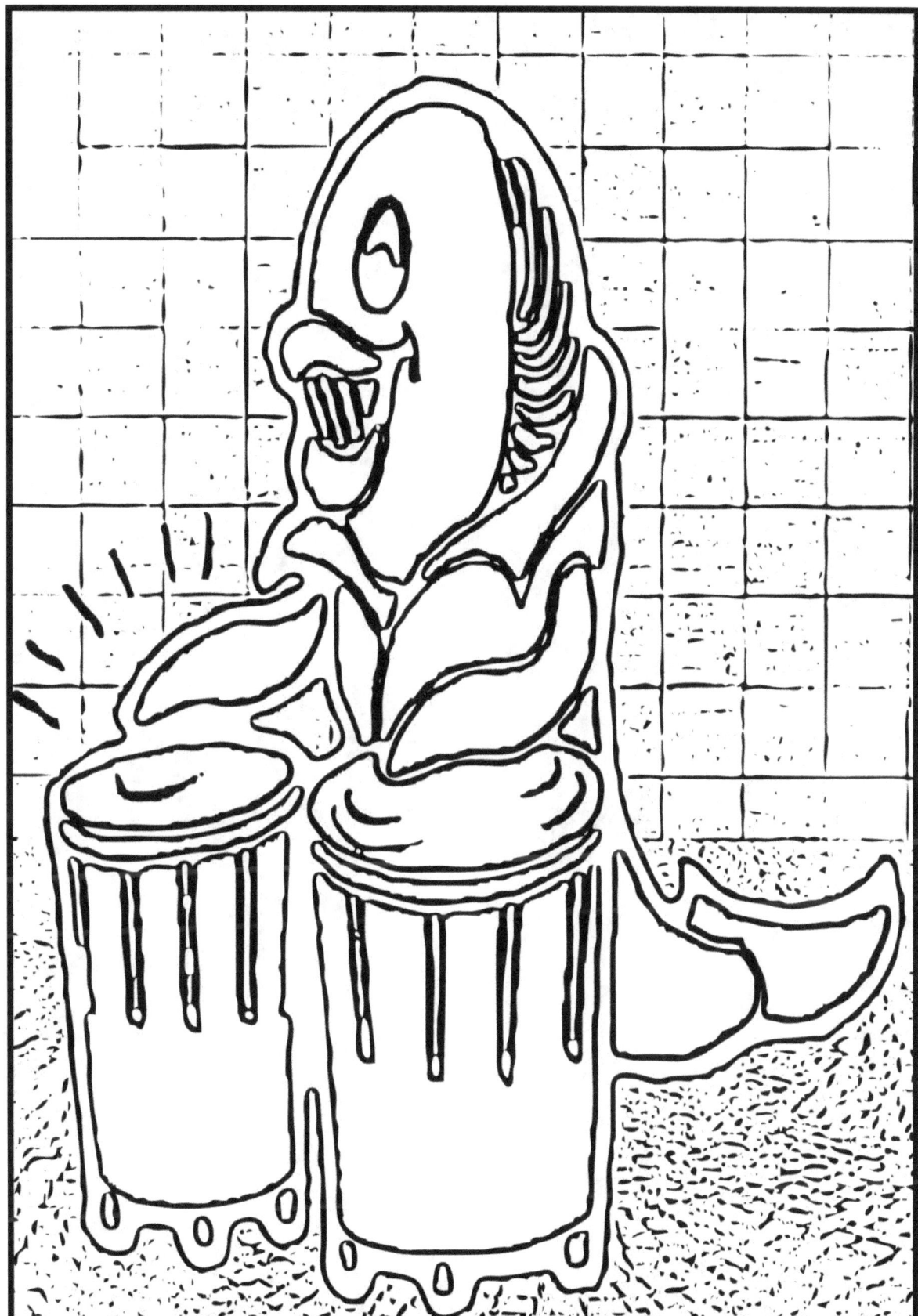

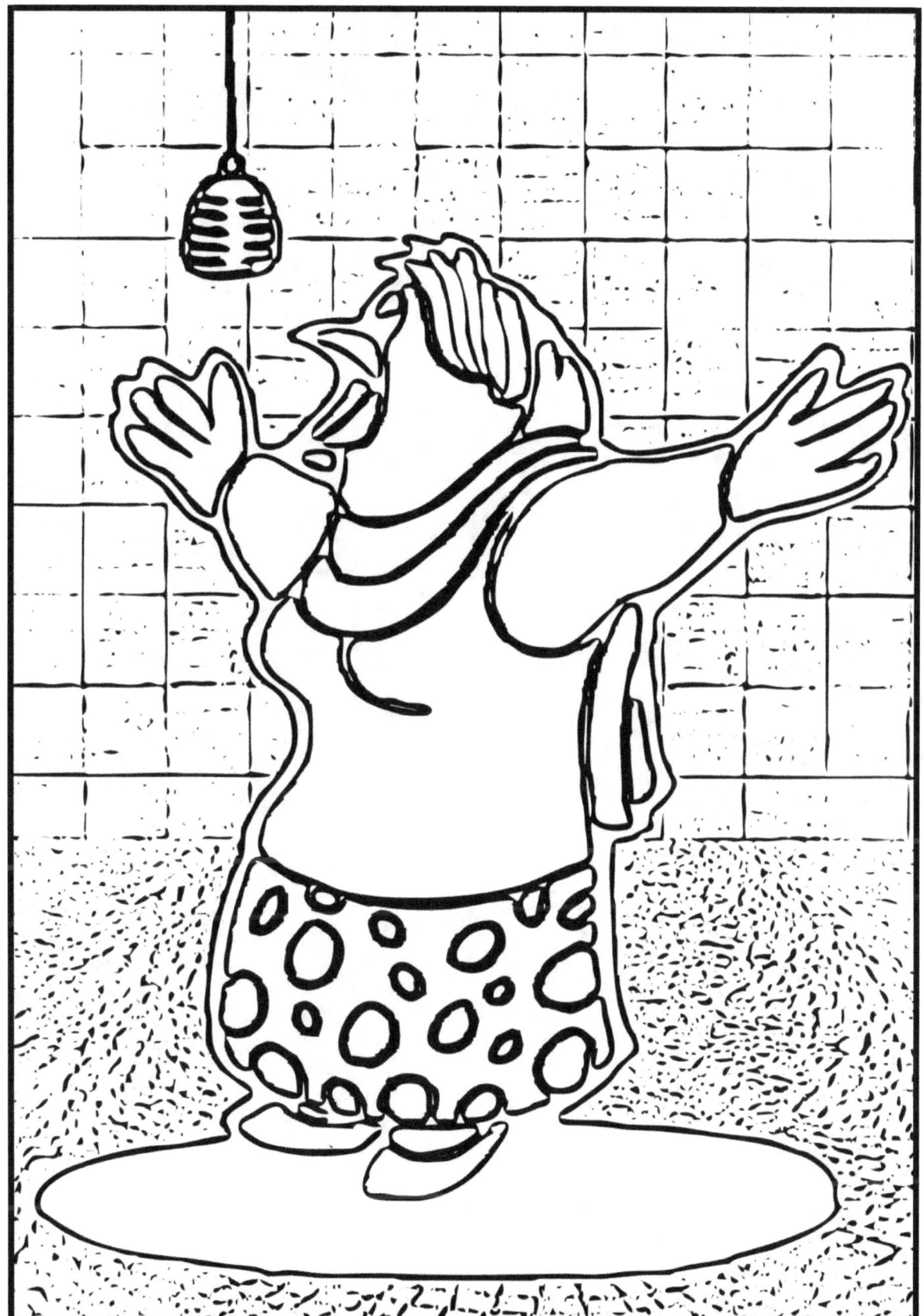

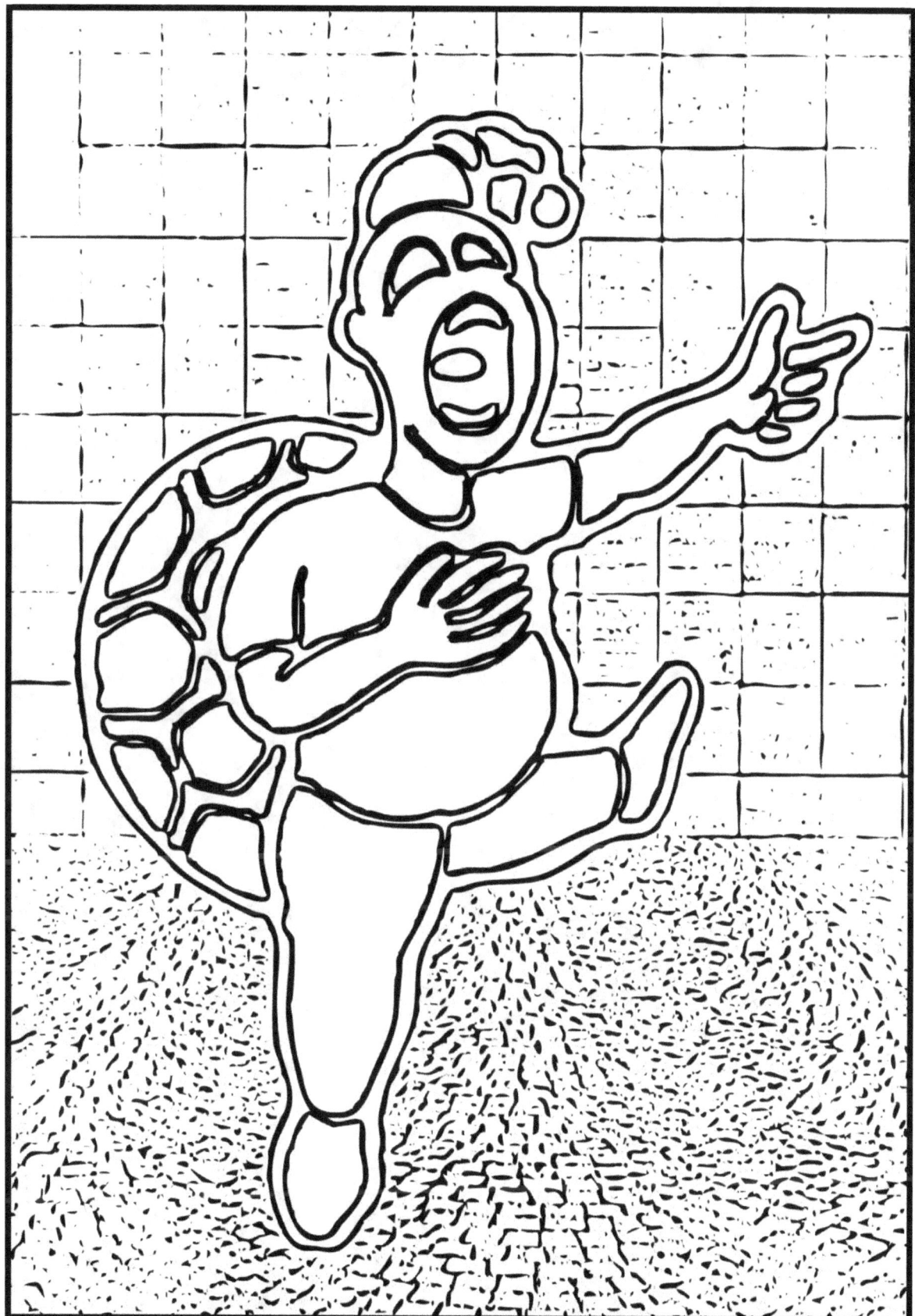

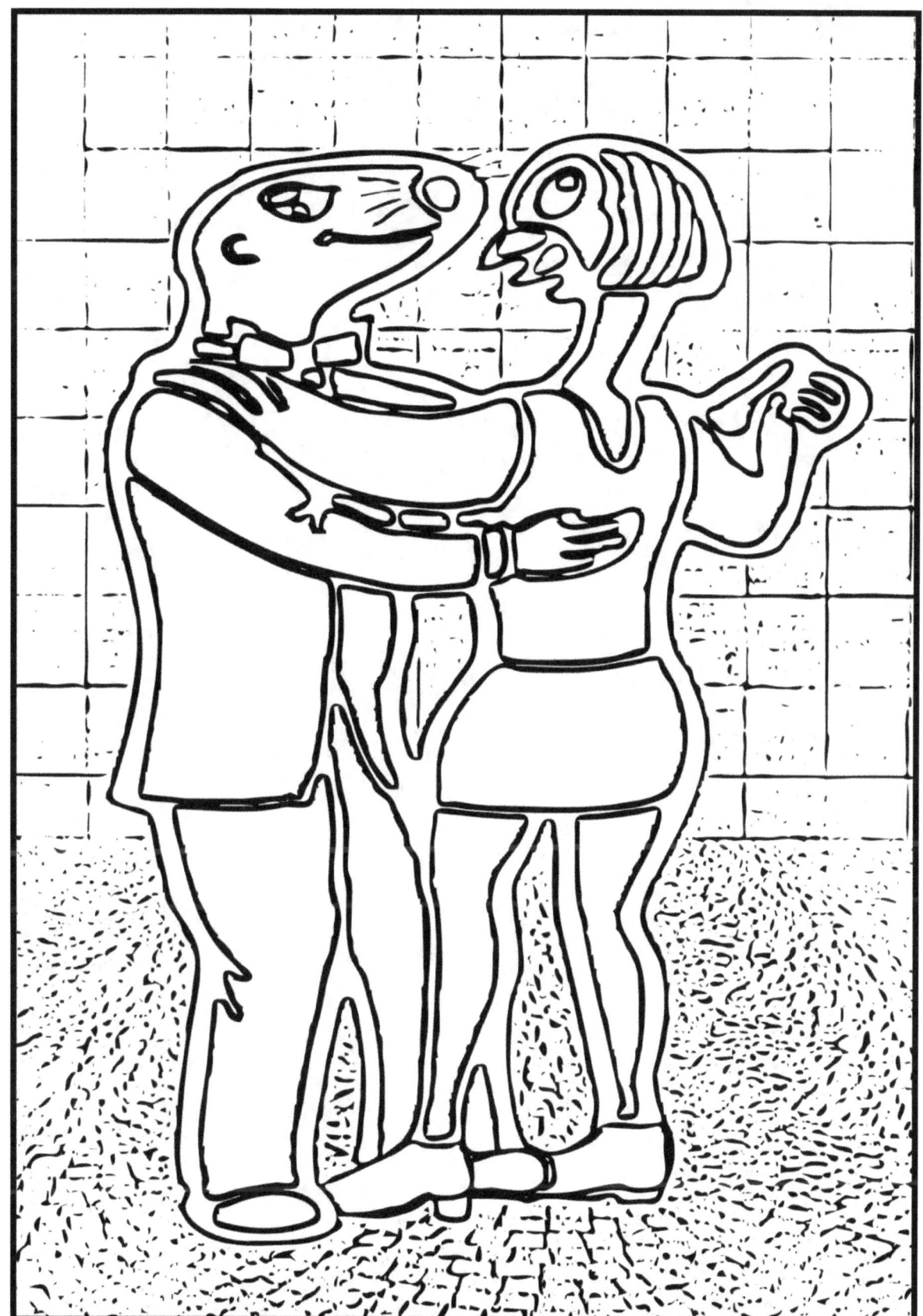

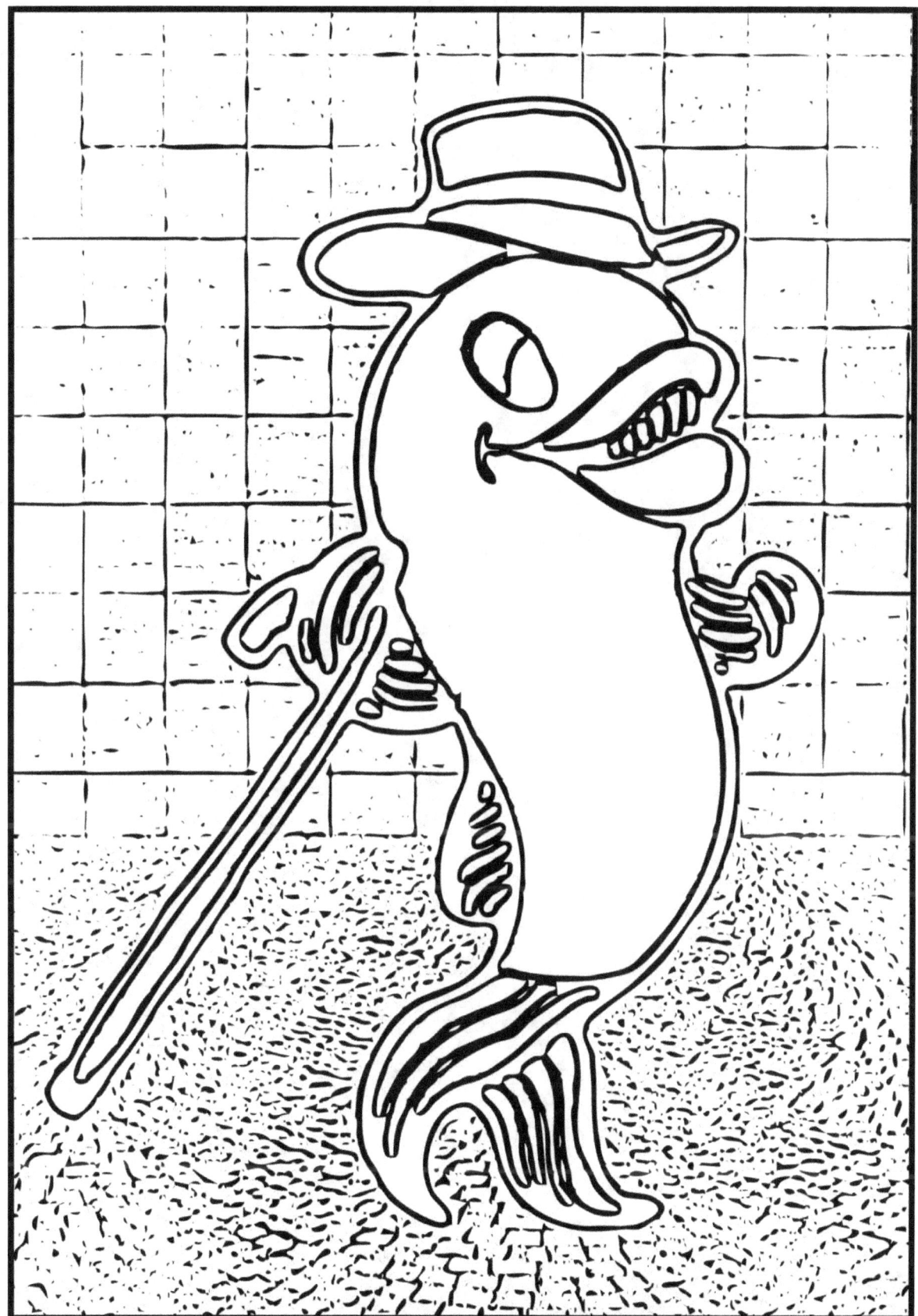

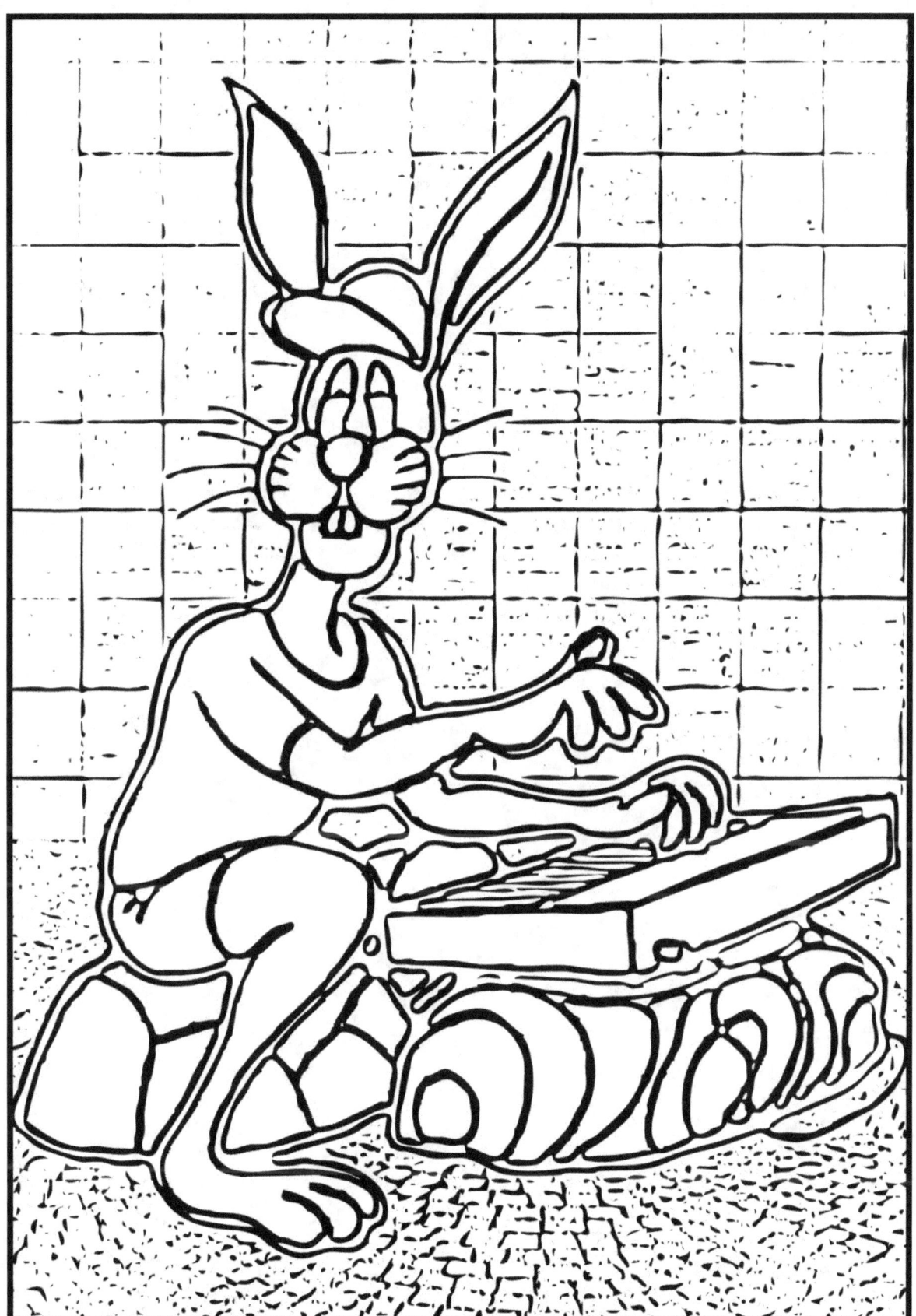

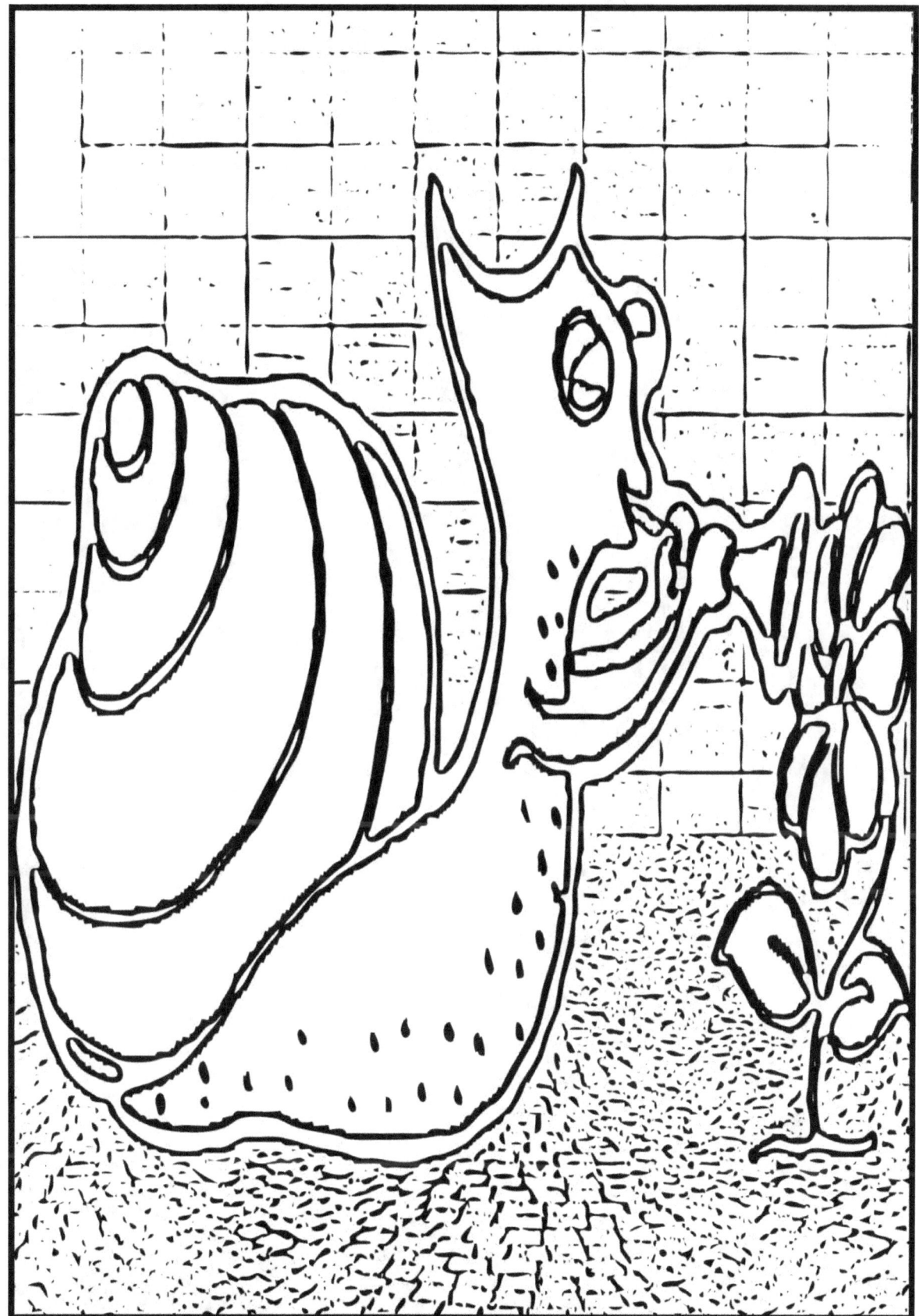

www.ingramcontent.com/pod-product-compliance
Lightning Source LLC
Chambersburg PA
CBHW081547170526
45166CB00009B/2606

* 9 7 8 1 5 2 2 7 8 4 9 8 2 *